PRAISES FOR ULTIMATE SACRIFICE

"Bishop Joe Kwapong, in his new book Ultimate Sacrifice, has dug deep into the rich soil of divine revelation and given fresh eyes to an ancient text about the Patriarch Abraham's willingness to sacrifice that which he loved the most—his son Isaac—on the altar of obedience to God… you will be inspired and enriched as you walk through these pages and apply these truths to your heart."

Dr. James J. Seymour
North Haven Church
Saint Augustine's University

"I have known Bishop Joe Kwapong for nearly 40 years, and have closely observed his passion for God which he has exhibited in the work of the Ministry and in service to humanity…*Ultimate Sacrifice* is a masterpiece…I endorse and recommend it."

Bishop Samuel C. Fuah
Senior Presiding Bishop
Love Fellowship of Churches and Ministries

"This book—Ultimate Sacrifice—reveals the meaning of worship and the different forms of worship in a way that will completely make you question the adequacy of your worship or sacrifice to God… The choice of words, the research, the intricate nature of syntax employed in the writing of this book is what makes it informative and fun to read. Bravo Bishop Kwapong!"

Dr. Richard Ayi
Chief Operating Officer
Global Infectious Disease Services, PC

"This book is an encounter with God and a journey which reveals the true essence of worship. It is a compelling must-read for every Christian…"

Dr. Bertha Serwa Ayi, (MD, FACP, FIDSA, MBA)
CEO/ Medical Director
Global Infectious Disease Services, PC

"…Bishop Joe Kwapong's book—*Ultimate Sacrifice*—is both timely and compelling, especially at a time when many in the church are gradually losing sight of the spiritual meaning and significance of sacrifice… by tracing the spiritual meaning and significance of sacrifice to the Old Testament and foreshadowing it to the sacrifice of Christ in the New Testament, readers get a complete and seamless account of the concept and application of sacrifice rather than in snapshots."

Dr. Joseph P. Eshun Jr. (Ph.D.)
Associate Professor
East Stroudsburg University, PA.

"Bishop Joe Kwapong brings us back to what really matters in our Christian pilgrimage-WORSHIP. From his carefully thought out and researched book, he reminds us that there can be no true worship without sacrifice. In a day of self-gratification, many are missing the true essence of giving their all to God. It is time for the worshippers to arise, let them arise and offer their sacrifices to God who gave the *Ultimate Sacrifice* in His Son. Let's all emulate King David who brought a costly sacrifice and declared, "I'll never offer to God an offering that costs me nothing...This is a book that will bring a worship revolution in the Body of Christ. More Grace!"

Dr. Frank Ofosu-Appiah
Living Springs International Churches
All Nations Church. Atlanta GA
Advanced Life Ministries.

Ultimate Sacrifice

Worship At The Place Called There

JOE KWAPONG

Ultimate Sacrifice

Worship At The Place Called There

JOE KWAPONG
Faith Revival Publishing, LLC
Atlanta, Georgia 30084. U.S.A

ULTIMATE SACRIFICE by Joe Kwapong. Copyright © 2016 by Faith Revival Publishing, LLC. All Rights Reserved.

PUBLISHED BY: FAITH REVIVAL PUBLISHING, LLC
A Division of Faith Revival Mission International, Inc. USA.
4901-A South Royal Atlanta Drive, Tucker, GA 30084.
Telephone: 1-888-494-4677

Cover Design by FIIFOS GRAPHIX CONCEPTS, LLC
Cover Design copyright © 2016 by Fiifos Graphix Concepts, LLC.
All Rights Reserved.

No part of this publication may be reproduced, stored in retrieval system or transmitted in any way by any means, electronic, mechanical, photocopy, recording or otherwise without the prior permission of the author except as provided by USA copyright laws. All Scripture quotations are taken from The Holy Bible. All Rights Reserved.

This book is designed to provide accurate and authoritative information with regard to the subject matter covered. This information is given with the understanding that neither the author nor Faith Revival Publishing is engaged in rendering legal, professional advice. Since the details of your situation are fact dependent, you should additionally seek the services of a competent professional.

Library of congress cataloging in publication data.

ISBN: 978-0-692-84822-7

Printed in the United States of America.

This book and all other Faith Revival Publishing, LLC books are available at special discounts when purchased in bulk by corporations, organizations, and special-interest groups. For information, please contact fiifos@yahoo.com or call 1-888-494-4677.

DEDICATION

Firstly, I dedicate this book to the Body of Christ. My prayer is that it will unleash a new wave of sacred worship and uninhibited praise across the nations.

Secondly, I dedicate it to my wife Lady Vicky and, my daughters—Adrielle and Cheryl.

I also dedicate it to my mother Mama Agnes Rita Kwapong, and my mother-in-law; Mommy Ernestina Bright-Davies. To my siblings, their spouses and children: Bishop Eric Kwapong, Eric Ayeyi and Rachel; Mrs. Marian & Rev. David Baines, Ernie and Michael; Dr. Mrs. Mercy & Dr. Martin Maclean, Medric, Jaime and Denise; Mrs. Mina and Rev. Paa Nii Tackie, Amanda, Christine, Michael, and Hillary; and Mr. Emmanuel Afriyie Kwapong.

To my brothers-in-law, their spouses and children: Rev. Tom & Cece Bright-Davies, Karen, Stacy, Tometta, and Kelly Ann; Mr. Benjamin and Edinam Bright-Davies, Joel, Jude, Benjamin Jr, and Anna-Jo.

Lastly, to all music pastors who play the dual role of leading the congregation in word, music or song, I know how demanding your job is. You deserve double honor for your work's sake. This one is for you!

ACKNOWLEDGEMENT

I would like to thank the following people, who helped make this dream of writing this book a reality. The truth is, without your encouragement and support, this book would have remained a pipe-dream. You are proof that *"it takes teamwork to make the dream work."* From the depths of my heart, I am eternally grateful.

First and foremost, to my Lord and Savior Jesus Christ, who so loved me that He shed His blood for my redemption and justification.

To Lady Vickie, my life-long comrade, confidant and companion, who helped with organizing my thoughts, and continue to support my every endeavor, I am forever indebted to you.

To Benjamin Tee Bright-Davies, I am grateful for making the time to proof-read and edit this book. Also to Dr. Bertha Serwa Ayi, who made time not only to proof-read, and edit, but also write the book summary (back cover), I am eternally grateful.

To my daughters Adrielle and Cheryl; my biggest fans who believed in me so much. You were willing to invest your college funds and personal money in this project! That was mind-blowing.

To my nephew Eric Ayeyi Ako Kwapong and niece Rachel Inshira Kwapong, who supported me with millennia lingo, dictation and encouragement—I am thankful.

To Bishop Eric O. Kwapong, I am appreciative of your encouragement, and for the foreword.

To Dr. Anedi Gisela Eme-Akwari and your children; Onyekwere, Ngozi, and Okechukwu; you have been a rock to my family. I am appreciative of your support. I am eternally grateful.

To Rev. Morris Appiah, Rev. Kofi Okyere, Minister Tricia Reindorf (Botchway), Rev. Sammy Awuku-Gyekye, (Mrs. Edith Brako and Mrs. Herty Odamtten—of blessed memory), Sabina Wood, Ruby Odamtten, Dorothy Johnson, Sylvia Ofori-Boadu, Minister Esther Barnes, Mrs. Tina Clinton Hammond, Mrs. Ida Opare-Ayensu, Rev. Alex Ampiaw—my covenant brothers and sisters of Judah-Praise International. We ate *kenkey and fish*, prayed and practiced for hours on end, and had fun doing it.

Last but certainly not the least, I am grateful to my publisher, Faith Revival Publishing, LLC for a job well done.

TABLE OF CONTENTS

Dedication		ix
Acknowledgement		xi
Foreword		14
Introduction		17
Chapter 1	Obedience In Worship	24
Chapter 2	Sensitivity In Worship	39
Chapter 3	Preparation In Worship	56
Chapter 4	Going Deeper	70
Chapter 5	Setting The Stage	81
Chapter 6	Father And Son	97
Chapter 7	Building An Altar	111
Chapter 8	The Ultimate Sacrifice	124
Chapter 9	Divine Provision in Worship	137
Chapter 10	Angelic Visitation	150
Chapter 11	God Reciprocates	164
Chapter 12	Finale	179

FOREWORD

The entirety of our relationship with God is pivoted on the truth of the total submission of our lives to Jesus Christ as Lord of our lives and not just Savior and Redeemer.

We are called upon and enjoined by the Holy Scriptures and teachings of our Lord Jesus Christ to embrace and make the subject matter of sacrifice our thinking and lifestyle, and thereby live the true worship life of Christ.

Living by the principles of sacrifice is not a simple and easy path to walk, whether it is in the context of developing and enriching our faith and spirituality, or strengthening good values of life.

The principles of sacrifice will most of the time make varied degrees of extremely-strenuous demands on our commitments in human relationships and efforts to deepen our knowledge and experience of God and enrich our spirituality.

In the very beginning, man was created perfect with true understanding of sacrifice. It has always been the foundation of the Christian faith and man's relationship with the Lord Jesus Christ. However, since the fall of man, the purity and understanding of true sacrifice has been lost and therefore man's desire to deeply appreciate and live the life of sacrifice to enrich his spirituality and enhance his life's values is also greatly undermined.

Our Lord Jesus Christ came to give His life a ransom for our salvation, and thereby in the process He demonstrated and restored the understanding and appreciation of the principle of sacrifice as a lifestyle.

The sad reality is that, today, this subject matter which seriously enriches and principally holds in place our spirituality while enhancing our life's values has been completely relegated to the background and is treated as insignificant.

However, Bishop Joe Kwapong, in his book *Ultimate Sacrifice*, presents refreshing exposure and engages different perspectives of this critically important truth of sacrifice in a way that reaffirms it as the most important bedrock of our Christian faith.

His historical and in-depth exploration of this subject provides the reader with the understanding, as well as practical and spiritual insights that make the lifestyle of sacrifice an enriching and rewarding worship experience.

Joe Kwapong exegetically presents enriching theological perspectives, and further strengthens the case that sacrifice is the foundation and very life of true worship.

His discourse is based on Abraham's attempted sacrifice of his son Isaac in Genesis 22, and shows this as the real story of God our Heavenly Father offering His dear son Jesus Christ, and that sacrifice is synonymous with worship.

This means that one cannot truly worship God without strongly appreciating and living the life of holy sacrifice as we see in the example of our Lord Jesus Christ in His Ultimate Sacrifice of giving His life as a ransom for our salvation and worship to His Father God.

This great book is definitely a must-read for all.

-Bishop Eric Oduro Kwapong

INTRODUCTION

TO SACRIFICE IS TO GIVE UP—surrender, forfeit or renounce—something of great value, for the purpose of achieving something else perceived as being of much greater value.[1] [2]

For instance, to give up an hour of sleep for more study time to achieve academic excellence is a sacrifice.

However, to make the *ultimate sacrifice* is to give up anything of incalculable value including one's life, for an even greater cause; a concept our men and women in uniform are familiar with.

Although not categorically stated, I would argue that the record of God making coats of skin to cover Adam and his wife Eve after the fall was the first ***sense*** of sacrificing an animal for the liberation of sinful humankind. (Ref. Genesis 3:21)

---

[1] ©2017 Oxford University Press
www.oxforddictionaries.com/definition/sacrifice
[2] ©2017 Merriam-Webster Incorporated
www.merriam-webster.com/dictionary/sacrifice

Then there were brothers Cain and Abel who gave an offering to the Lord. The scripture says,
Abel "killed the first-born lamb from one of his sheep and gave the Lord the best parts of it. The Lord was pleased with Abel and his offering." (Ref. Genesis 4:4)

Also, Noah after the flood offered the first burnt offering to the Lord. Surprisingly, something spectacularly compelling about Noah's sacrifice produced sweet savory aromatherapy, attractive enough to literally entice God to have a "change of heart," never again to destroy the world with water.

TWO INSEPARABLE REALITIES

The Apostle Paul wrote to the Church at Rome of two inseparable realities...*sacrifice and worship*. "Therefore, I urge you, brothers and sisters, in view of God's mercy, to offer your bodies as a living sacrifice, holy and pleasing to God--this is your true and proper worship." -Romans 12:1

In this modern day and age of contemporary worship, God still requires sacrifice. The stark reality is that, these two are inseparable. To worship is to offer sacrifice; to offer sacrifice is to worship

Whereas we no longer offer costly animal sacrifice, God has never changed, nor will He relent in demanding the same level of quality, purity, selfless devotion and unflinching commitment to His worship.

WORSHIP

The word *"worship"* appears 108 times in the King James Version of the Bible. Having read its first mention in Genesis 22, I discovered to my surprise it had absolutely no involvement with singing, the playing of any musical instruments, or a praise-break; in contemporary terms, "getting your praise on."

How could this account speak to a worship experience without any singing? I pondered with much difficulty.

Being the very first passage to mention worship, I thought the depiction of how it was executed was paramount, seeing it could possibly be the model to set the tone for the rest of the scriptures. However, it was nothing like I anticipated.

THE JOURNEY

In response to God's order to get into the land of Moriah, to offer his son Isaac as a burnt offering on one of the mountains—His Ultimate Sacrifice—

Abraham embarked on the three-day pilgrimage, along with Isaac and two young men from his household.

In a greater likelihood, these young men were menservants, as Abraham kept servants who managed his estate and entertained his guests.

Upon arrival at the place, Abraham instructed the two to stay with the donkey, while he and his son went farther to *worship* and return to them. (Genesis 22:5)

The Hebrew word translated as *worship* in the text is *shachah* which means *"to bow down."*

ACCEPTABLE MODEL

Everything—starting with the instructions God gave to Abraham regarding sacrificing his son Isaac; to the manner in which he responded, up until God intervened and changed the initial instruction—encapsulates what I consider to be the enduring truth and principles regarding the acceptable model for offering the Ultimate Sacrifice to God.

THE 5 ELEMENTS OF TRUE WORSHIP

Some of the key revelations I highlight in this book include what I caption; *"the 5 elements of true worship."*

These are principles which were imperative, if indeed Abraham was going to effectively execute God's orders in Moriah—having arrived after a 3-day pilgrimage to the holy place of worship.

These principles hold true even till this day, and have a direct correlation with how to worship properly.

First is the *WOOD,* which was for the burnt offering.

We can draw a parallel on its significance and how that relates to the New Testament era.

Then there is ISAAC, the *Ultimate Sacrifice* Abraham was willing to offer as burnt offering to God—without hesitation or reservation.

Next, I discuss the *FIRE* and its significance—which was to ignite and consume the sacrifice, without which there would be no smoke to ascend to heaven. Further, I talk about the *KNIFE,* which was to slay the animal being sacrificed.

Finally, the ultimate sacrifice had to be placed on an *ALTAR*, before being consumed by the fire.

For each one of these *"elements"* I offer an in-depth interpretation.

Now I quite understand that not everyone who reads this book will necessarily agree with my interpretation, but I think it is worth pondering over the argument that drew me to my conclusion.

I also believe that worship is innate, and that humankind was created to offer worship to our Creator. Since worship is innate, I would argue that it is only a matter of course before we begin to offer worship to the object of our admiration.

While some may offer worship to a deity, others have their object of worship being wealth, family heritage or even celebrities.

Again, I believe you will be tremendously impacted as we closely examine Abraham's actions from the time God instructed him to offer Isaac at Moriah on a mountain he was going to tell him of, to the time God intervened and redirected Abraham to a ram that had been trapped in the bushes nearby.

It is my prayer that you will be impacted as much as I have, in fostering a deeper walk with God—in a manner only the Holy Spirit can ignite.

You will discover that many times, worship has very little to do with music, although music is a medium through which we express praise and worship.

My motivation in writing this book has been driven by the divine revelation from an insightful exposé of this captivating story.

In Matthew's gospel chapter 16:13-17, the author records Jesus coming into the coasts of Caesarea Philippi, and asking his disciples whom people professed him to be.

After telling Jesus some perceived him to be John the Baptist, while others thought he was Elijah or Jeremiah, Jesus asked His disciples directly, whom they thought He was.

"Simon Peter answered,
You are the Messiah, the Son of the living God"- Matthew 16:16 (NIV)
To which Jesus answered,
"Blessed are you Simon son of Jonah, for this was not revealed to you by flesh and blood, but by my Father in heaven." (Matthew 16:17 NIV)

There is therefore such a thing as receiving divinely-inspired information from God.

The litmus test is that, for the most part, it will not contradict the plenary inspired word of God.

Chapter 1
OBEDIENCE IN WORSHIP

"And it came to pass after these things that God did tempt Abraham and said unto him, Abraham: and he said, Behold, here I am. And he said, take now thy son, your only son Isaac whom thou love, and get thee into the land of Moriah." –Genesis 22:1-2a.

After reading this text for the first time, my thoughts were filled with a barrage of questions—allowing me no chance to gloss over the text. What did the writer mean by *"after these things"*?

Did God really tempt Abraham? Does the scripture not say,

"Let no man say when he is tempted, I am tempted of God: for God cannot be tempted with evil, neither tempts he any man:"? - James 1:13

As I prayerfully meditated on the scriptures, looking up original words in Hebrews and cross-referencing scriptures, I read a passage of scripture which states;

"Howbeit when He, the Spirit of truth, is come, He will guide you into all the truth: for He shall not speak of himself; but whatsoever He shall hear, that shall he speak: and he will show you things to come." – John 16:13

AFTER THESE THINGS

This phrase referred to the aftermath of the entire saga of God visiting (the then) Abram—whose name meant "high father" in Hebrew. This was a reflection and depiction of his degenerate condition, or to put it objectively moderate livelihood. Proceeding after this was the change of his name to Abraham (which meant "father of many") to reflect the blessing as a result of his encounter with Yahweh, the Creator of the universe.

"After these things" also meant after Abraham and his wife had been cured of their barrenness, and rewarded with their son Isaac—after waiting for God's promise of a son for nearly 25 years. Basically, during the time when Abraham had gone from living fairly moderately, to the point where after his encounter with God, he had become the envy of his community.

To put this in modern-day lingo, Abraham was now living-large. It was after all these things that God decides to test Abraham's loyalty.

The life-lesson here is, it is imperative that we always remember who is behind our success and well-being. Many a time, most of us remain humble, and constantly remember to rely and depend on God for help, as long as we have a sense of inadequacy.

The real question however is, will we maintain that same attitude of dependency and reliance on God, if by the stroke of divine favor, things took a turn for the better?

There is always a greater likelihood of forgetting to remain humble, and not remembering the times of little beginnings.

The Ultimate Sacrifice involves never forgetting that the same God who makes all grace abound to us, has the exclusive right to demand our all, whenever He deems fit.

We should always remember the admonition of the scriptures, which states:
"The blessing of the Lord makes a person rich and He adds no sorrow with it." – Proverbs 10:22 (NLT)

This scripture affirms the fact that it is the blessing of the Lord that produces prosperity, and not just hard work alone.

GOD TEMPTED ABRAHAM

The scripture refutes the suggestion that God tempts humankind. It clearly states that;

"Let no man say when he is tempted, I am tempted of God: for God cannot be tempted with evil, neither tempts he any man." - James 1:13

Therefore, the scripture establishes the fact that God does not tempt us; neither can He be tempted with evil. To tempt is to entice to do evil. This is diametrically opposed to the nature of God.

The Hebrew word translated as "tempt" is Nasah; which means to test, prove, try, or to put to the test.[3]

Testing in this instance is to investigate the quality of someone or something, through the demonstration of stress.

Usually the objective for conducting stress tests is to test for durability and sustainability.

Therefore, it is clear, given everything that has been stated, that God had no vested interest in tempting Abraham, or anyone else for that matter.

---

[3]NAS Exhaustive Concordance
http://biblehub.com/hebrew/5254.htm
©2004-2016

After all, it was He who blessed Abraham, and gave him all his wealth including a son.

The experience was meant to test Abraham's character, so as to be refined through testing. Remember the Hebrew word translated as *"tempt"* means to ***test.***

Moreover, by 1611 AD, when the King James Version of the Hebrew bible was translated, the word "nasah" was wrongly translated as tempt, which means "to entice to do evil" rather than test.

Everyone who has gone through school has had to go through various tests at different stages of their education in order to be promoted.

Usually when you fail a test, it implies that you are not prepared for the next level. Whoever overlooks poor performance and promotes anyway, does that to the detriment of the object or person being tested.

Imagine a car that fails a crash-test, but is put on the market anyway for sales. Many lives will be at risk.

Yet, I know certain Christians and leaders who are yet to be tested through the school of hard knocks and "street-ology," defined by me as "the successful survival in street-smartness, when stuck between a rock and a hard place."

Ultimate Sacrifice — Joe Kwapong

In my life as a young minister of the gospel, I remember praying to God to use me as He did with stalwart ministers such as Oral Roberts, Aimee Semple McPherson, Dr. Myles Monroe, Morris Cerullo, T. L. Osborn, Kathryn Kuhlman and the like.

What I failed to realize was that these men and women had been tried and tested.

Question is; am I able to handle the high level of stress they had to deal with?

In a similar fashion, I know certain schools and colleges who overlook poor academic performance, to admit gifted athletes whose academic performance do not necessarily match their sports ability. In the long run, they may excel in sports, but will struggle in academia.

It makes complete sense therefore, that God would allow Abraham to be tested in order to prove his loyalty and dependability on God; especially at a time when he and his wife seemed to be living comfortably.

They had crossed the bridge of waiting in limbo for twenty-five years for a son, and were enjoying life.

Everything was hunky-dory!

Whenever you are tempted, just remember that God wants to allow you to be tested in order for you to prove your durability and loyalty. This is the test for your promotion.

There is never a hidden agenda on God's part to entice you to do evil.

Furthermore, the scripture says,
"There is no temptation that has overtaken man, but such as is common to everyman. But God can be trusted not to let you be tempted above what you can handle, and even with that, God will show you how to escape from that temptation." – 1 Corinthians 10:13

Now, tell me if that is not awesome!

TAKE NOW THY SON

The instruction to offer his Ultimate Sacrifice was first captured in these four simple words. Clearly non-negotiable and somewhat unsettling, I would have wondered where all this was leading to had I been Abraham.

I would ask, "What now?" And probably to ignore the unreasonable demand, I would dismiss it as some demonic influence to rob me of my inheritance.

So "take now," God says. Which meant, take without reservation or hesitation. Do not give it any thought or consideration even if it made no sense to you. Do it now!

Therefore, in the *ultimate sacrifice*, we offer now, without reservation or hesitation.

The scripture says,

"He who observes the wind won't sow; and he who regards the clouds won't reap." - Ecclesiastes 11:4 (W.E.B)

This means, you could have a thousand reasons not to offer your treasure, talent or time to God, if you wanted to find one.

Next He says "thy son."

In today's phraseology, we would say: God did not stutter. God was not mincing words. He came to Abraham with specificity, and needed his most-prized possession at the place called there, if Abraham was to have a true worship encounter.

Did this depiction of God giving an emphatic command without regard for sensitivity to the needs of poor Abraham not seem out of character?

Was he unaware that Abraham had suffered long enough? Why come to him now to unsettle him? One thing I can attest to is that the older we get, the more settled we become.

Therefore, to come to this old man at this point of his life to make this demand had to have been unwelcome, I could imagine.

However, the lesson here is to know that to offer the Ultimate Sacrifice at the place called there, we ought to know in the lingo of good old King James that; *"we are not of our own,"* and that God owns us, and has the exclusive right to demand anything of us, and to do as He pleases with us.

The scripture says,
"For by him were all things created, that are in heaven, and that are in earth, visible and invisible, whether they be thrones, or dominions, or principalities, or powers: all things were created by him, and for him." - (Colossians 1:16)

Similarly, our purpose for being created was predetermined by Him and not by us. We all showed up on the world stage with predetermined giftings, and special abilities we had no hand in.

Therefore, to offer the *ultimate sacrifice* is to yield our all to Him in obedience, knowing that our Creator has the exclusive right to mandate as He pleases with us.

The challenge, however, is most of us from the "free-world" resent any form of infringement on our liberty and freedom.

We frown on dictatorship, and storm the streets in protest against any attempt to take away our amendment rights.

As much as this is our inalienable right, the *ultimate worship* is the uninhibited submission of our rights to God the Father, Christ our Savior, and the Holy Spirit our advocate, as an act of our will without coercion.

I believe God demands instant and complete obedience, even in our worship. Partial obedience or delayed obedience is incomplete obedience, and does not attract God's optimum blessing.

Secondly, just as God commanded Abraham to "take now thy son," we too as children of God, must learn to listen for instructions in worship.

Sometimes the instructions may come from the worship leader, but then whenever we take the time to prepare before the worship encounter, God will instruct us directly.

I know certain "big" bishops and prestigious apostles who will not participate in corporate worship, let alone take instructions from the worship leader. God is never silent in true worship. He speaks, and gives directions.

Let's learn the art of listening and obeying God in worship.

THINE ONLY SON ISAAC WHOM YOU LOVE.

It does not get any more specific than this. The Hebrew word translated as "love" here, is "Ahab"- meaning "to have affection for" (as in beloved, dearly love, or lover).[4]

Evidently, God was not just asking Abraham for a son. Rather, He was specifically asking for Abraham's son Isaac, whom he had affection for; a son who meant the world to his dad.

If this is a standard to go by, then I submit to you that for a lot of what we call "anointed praise and worship" God is not pleased at all.

Remember God Himself sacrificed His only begotten son Jesus Christ, whom He had affection for.

Growing up in Africa, my siblings and I always attended Sunday school with a penny as our offering. For those of us from the old-school, we know it as "silver-collection."

We were taught that poverty was the servitude of love, and to further affirm this paradigm, we were

---

[4] Strong's Exhaustive Concordance
www.biblehub.com © 2004-2016 by Bible Hub

taught songs that affirmed that God had no objection with the quality of our offering.

Not only did I find that to be untrue as I got older and searched the scriptures for myself, I wonder how my parents could have bought into this preposterous fabrication.

The first passage of scripture to have ever recorded humans offering sacrifice to God, was in Genesis chapter 4, when two brothers—Cain and Abel—both brought offerings to God.

Cain's offering was rejected by God, while Abel's was accepted.

A close study of the text reveals that, Cain was in total violation of the rules of engagement, hence his offering being rejected.

This whole argument gives credibility to the fact that the quality of your seed before engaging Yahweh in the place of worship is critically important.

Secondly, in the true worship encounter with God, we must offer him our Isaac, whom we love! Your Isaac represents your life—the best of your time, talent, and treasure; body, soul and spirit! God does not just receive junk as worship. He is worthy of your very best.

He was not being unreasonable when He demanded Isaac, whom Abraham and his wife had labored for so long to give birth to.

Instead, I think God was establishing the fact that to offer the *ultimate sacrifice* at the place called there, our sacrifice must be stellar and of the highest quality.

GET INTO THE LAND OF MORIAH

"Mount Moriah in old city Jerusalem is the site of numerous biblical acts of faith. It is also one of the most-valuable and hotly-contested pieces of real estate on earth.

This is a profoundly sacred area to Christians, Jews, and Muslims. Sitting atop Mount Moriah today is the Temple Mount, a 37-acre tract of land where the Jewish temple once stood.

Several important Islamic holy sites are there now, including the Dome of the Rock – a Muslim shrine built thirteen hundred years ago – and the Al-Aqsa Mosque."[5]

The pilgrimage to Moriah had to be a journey taken by faith. On the one hand, although Abraham

---

[5] www.gotquestions.org – Bible Questions Answered
©Copyright 2002-2016 Got Questions Ministries

had an idea where Moriah was, he had no clue where the specific spot was—where he was to offer his son as the burnt offering to God.

That spot after all was supposed to be his very final destination—the holy site where the encounter would take place.

Secondly, he was not privy to the fact that God's plan was to intervene and replace Isaac with a ram. The record will also show that Abraham's obedience to go to Moriah, to carry out God's orders, is what earned him the much-coveted place in history as the father of the three major religions of the world—Judaism, Christianity and Islam.

Everyone at some point in the course of their life will make a pilgrimage to Moriah. You will know of a "witness" in your heart—the need to turn on a new leaf, start a new business, write a book, poetry or a song, or even run for an elected office or to pursue further studies.

That journey would have to be one made by faith. The burning desire to embark on that journey may even be one with very scanty or not much details.

But Abraham teaches us to commit things into the hands of God, and to take the step of faith.

Only God knows the rewards and lessons others will glean from our obedience.

LESSON:

Offering the Ultimate Sacrifice to God is precipitated by absolute obedience. God's command to Abraham was for him to sacrifice his son Isaac at Moriah without compromise.

Anything other than complete compliance was disobedience, tantamount to forfeiture of God's intent to bless him.

As New Testament believers, our Ultimate Sacrifice begins with total obedience to the word of God. Whether it is striving to obey the Ten Commandments or walking in forgiveness, our dutiful obedience is better than sacrifice, and to harken than the fat of rams.

Chapter 2
SENSITIVITY IN WORSHIP
"And offer him there for a burnt offering upon one of the mountains which I will tell thee of."
--Gen 22:2b

WHEN GOD INSTRUCTED Abraham to "offer him there," He was referring to an unspecified place in Moriah, on top of one of the mountains He was later going to reveal to Abraham.

Two things worthy of note regarding this undisclosed location are:

1. Abraham needed to be sensitive to the leading of God, in order to discern the specific spot God wanted Isaac sacrificed.

This may be a very inappropriate story to illustrate this point, but think about a country willing to pay ransom for the release of kidnapped soldiers. The successful release of the hostages is predicated on following the instructions given by the captors.

Another example would be a bomb-squad trying to diffuse a ticking bomb, set to go off at a public place where lives may be in jeopardy. To succeed at this mission, steady hands, great expertise and sensitivity to the mission, would be the bare minimum requirement to handle the task.

2. The central theme of this book is derived from the undisclosed location which I refer to as "the place called there."

It may have been a physical location in the text, but it is also a place of preparation. Like the hostage situation, or the ticking time-bomb, there is no room for error, or compromising of the specific mountain on which the sacrifice had to be made.

Abraham had to deliver to the letter. Yet, believers today offer sacrifices anywhere they please, without seeking instructions on which mountain to offer their sacrifice.

The rhetorical question is; which mountain are we supposed to offer our sacrifices on? Are we supposed to climb up a mountain to offer our sacrifice? Where is the place called *there*? And how do we get there?

WHERE IS THERE?

To worship at the place called *there* is to come before God, first knowing that "He is," and that He "rewards those who diligently seek Him."

It is also to walk in forgiveness, remembering that the scripture says;
"For if you forgive others for their transgressions, your heavenly father will also forgive you." –
Matthew 6:14 (NASB)

Also, to worship at the place called *there*, is to be sensitive to the Spirit of God, just as Abraham did, in listening for directions during the time of worship. While all this is true, the following additional virtues also guarantee the manifestation of God, and they are;

BROKENNESS

The scripture says,
"The Lord is near to the brokenhearted, and saves the crushed in spirit." - Psalm 34:18 (ESV)

There are some experiences that occur in our lives that cause us to be more sincere in seeking God. During such times, we are able to offer true worship from the place of brokenness. David once prayed on such an occasion with these words;
"Create in me a clean heart, O God, and renew a right spirit within me." – Psalm 51:10

Later he said;

"The sacrifices of God are a broken spirit; a broken and contrite heart, O God, thou wilt not despise" - (Psalm 51:17).

CONSECRATION

"To consecrate is *to* make or declare something (typically a church) sacred; dedicate formally to a religious or divine purpose.
Ordain (someone) to a sacred office, typically that of bishop."[6]

However, in this context, offering worship from a place of consecration is for every believer in Christ. This is the basis for every spiritual encounter, also in direct correlation with the scriptures, which states: "I exhort you therefore, brethren, by the mercies of God, to present your bodies a living sacrifice, holy and acceptable to God, which is your reasonable service." - Romans 12:1

SELFLESS DEVOTION

To be selfless is "caring more about other people's needs and interests than about your own,"

---

[6] https://en.oxforddictionaries.com/definition/consecrate
Oxford living dictionaries. ©2017 Oxford University Press

while devotion is "loyalty and love or care for someone or something."[7]

To worship at the place called *there* is to possess or to develop selfless devotion; first to God, then to humankind.

Abraham clearly put God's demand for his son, first, before considering his own. Clearly, he passed the test.

DEDICATION

Is defined as "the activity of giving a lot of your energy and time to something you think is important."[8]

People's perception on how important a thing is, is demonstrated by their actions. For example, to say you are dedicated to your job and keep showing up late is a contradiction.

If the job was that important, you would find a way to get there on time; just like Abraham's attitude to the place of worship. He rose up early, saddled his

---

[7] dictionary.cambridge.org/us/dictionary/English/selfless
Cambridge Academic Content Dictionary ©Cambridge University Press 2017

[8] dictionary.cambridge.org/us/dictionary/English/dedication
Cambridge Academic Content Dictionary ©Cambridge University Press 2017

donkey, got his act together and set out for the worship encounter.

HOLINESS

The primary meaning of holy is 'separate.' It comes from an ancient word that meant 'to cut,' or 'to separate.' God is uniquely holy, with no rivals or competition.[9]

As New Testament believers, the scripture admonishes us to be morally pure, which is also a part of our worship. To be holy is to be morally pure. To be morally pure is to be distinct from others. When writing to the Christians in Corinth, the apostle Paul states,

"Wherefore come out from among them, and be ye separate, says the Lord, and touch not the unclean thing; and I will receive you." – 2 Corinthians 6:17. We are not expected to be perfect, but to be distinct from the world. To worship at the place called *there* is to be separated from the world; it is to worship from the place of holiness.

---

[9] https://bible.org/seriespage/5-holiness-god
©2017 Bible.org

INTIMACY

Just as Jesus was the model of intimacy with God, because He and the Father are one, so we ought to seek to become one with God. - (Jn. 10:30)

"The noun "intimacy" comes from the Latin word "intimare" which means to "impress," or "make familiar," which comes from the Latin "intimus," meaning "inmost."[10]

God's idea of the creation of humankind was to foster an intimate relationship. This is evidenced in the Book of Genesis, where we read about the magnetic interaction between God, Adam and Eve. Consistently, God would make frequent stops at the couple's home, which was situated in a beautiful Garden with rare and exotic flowers, surrounded by turquoise-blue streams that wound its merry way through the garden.

A stroll through the beautiful garden was guaranteed to leave you feeling peaceful and "at-one" with the splendors of nature. It was at this attractive and picturesque garden that God would meet and share intimacy with the couple.

---

[10] https://www.vocabulary.com/dictionary/intimacy©Vocabulary.com

True worship creates the atmosphere where intimacy with God takes place, just as He intended it to be in the Garden of Eden.

ANTICIPATION

Defined as, "A feeling of excitement about something that is going to happen in the near future."[11]

Whenever we come into God's presence, we must come anticipating a move of God.

The move I am talking about is the exchange between divinity and humanity. We come with a worthy sacrifice; God approves our offering, and rewards us with His essence or being. His essence then produces whatever it is that we need.

Remember, there is nothing greater than His being—His manifest presence.

In Abraham's case, he was anticipating a sure Word of direction from heaven, to know which mountain to offer his sacrifice. Therefore, he needed to be sensitive to the voice of God.

By the same token, there is provision in His manifest presence, when we come anticipating to

---

[11]http://dictionary.Cambridge.org/us/dictionary/english/anticipation © Cambridge University Press. 2017

receive whatever we lack. You receive nothing when you have no expectation or anticipation, or are desensitized to the voice of God in the worship encounter.

BURNT OFFERING

Although not categorically stated, I would argue that the record of God making coats of skin to cover Adam and his wife Eve after the fall, gives us a sense of "burnt-offering" for the very first time. (Genesis 3:32)

Then there are those who hold that instead, the narrative fits better when Abel gave an offering to the Lord. The scripture says,
"And Abel, he also brought of the firstlings of his flock and of the fat thereof. And the Lord had respect unto Abel and to his offering." – Genesis 4:4

I guess one could infer from the text that, after killing the lamb, Abel must have offered it as a burnt-offering to the Lord.

However, the scriptures categorically state the account of Noah's burnt offering after the flood as the very first time burnt offerings were offered to God.
"The LORD smelled a sweet savor; and the LORD said in his heart, I will not again curse the ground any

more for man's sake; for the imagination of man's heart is evil from his youth; neither will I again smite any more everything living, as I have done." - Genesis 8:20

Surprisingly, something spectacularly compelling about Noah's burnt offering produced sweet savory aromatherapy, attractive enough to literally entice God to have a "change of heart."

This portion of scripture is unprecedented in that, there are very few instances in the Bible, where God seems to be wowed by human actions strong enough to get His undivided attention, resulting in Him having a change of heart!

Long after Noah's sacrifice, we know of Job's, then Jacob's, then the Passover sacrifice, to the Mosaic sacrifices in the Tabernacle and Temple.

BEYOND RECOGNITION

When a sacrifice is burnt, it is beyond recognition or reconstruction.

Therefore, one of the lessons we learn is that, when we present our Isaac before God—whether it is our time, talent, or treasure—we cannot keep record of it. We need to learn to let it go, as it is now beyond reclaim.

Ultimate Sacrifice — Joe Kwapong

I encourage you to get into the practice of offering spiritual sacrifices to God. When offered with a contrite, broken heart, or a grateful heart, God will always respond as He did Noah and Abraham. Under the New Testament, we do not offer sacrifices the way it was done under the Old.

The scripture asserts that;

"By him therefore let us offer the sacrifice of praise to God continually, that is, the fruit of our lips giving thanks to his name. But to do good and to communicate forget not: for with such sacrifices God is well pleased." – Hebrews 13:15 & 16

Clearly, we offer sacrifices "by Him" which is to say, for any sacrifice to be acceptable to God, it has to go through Christ. The shed blood of Jesus Christ on Calvary's cross was the epitome of the *Ultimate Sacrifice* that atoned for the sins of humankind.

No other burnt offering could surpass this sacrifice. Remember that God wrapped himself in human flesh as Christ, and sacrificed Himself for you and me.

Also, part of our sacrifice is showing mercy, and being kind-hearted; besides offering praise and thanksgiving.

God is well pleased with such sacrifices, the scripture says.

HISTORY OF BURNT OFFERING

As has been pointed out, the history of the burnt offering dates back to the days of Noah, although there is a great possibility that Abel's offering was a burnt offering.

The Hebrew word for "burnt offering" means to "ascend" or to "go up in smoke."[12]

God gave strict orders to Moses, regarding the sons of Aaron who were consecrated as priests and said;

"And he shall skin the burnt offering and cut it into its pieces... put fire on the altar, and lay the wood in order on the fire." – Leviticus 1:6-7b (AMPC)

In addition, God further instructed that Aaron's sons, lay the animal's head, and the fat in order on the wood which was on the altar, while its intestines and legs were first washed with water and placed on the altar as a burnt offering.

---

[12]http://www.google.com/amp/s/www.gotquestions.org/amp/burnt-offering.html?client ©Cambridge 2002-2016 Got Questions Ministries – Bible questions answered

The animal being sacrificed had to be a male sheep, bull, goat, turtledove or pigeon without any defect.

The priest was to slaughter it at the entrance of the tabernacle, drain the blood and sprinkle it at the altar. Specific animals were to be offered at specified times, depending on the occasion.

For instance, at the time of the Passover, the Israelites were to offer two young bulls, one ram, and seven lambs in their first year. These animals absolutely had to be without blemish.

In this day and age of contemporary worship, the Body of Christ has "evolved" with all kinds of "worship."

The stark reality is that, whereas we no longer offer animals as sacrifice, God has never changed nor will He relent in demanding the same level of quality, purity, selfless devotion and unflinching commitment to His worship. The problem is never with the style as it is with the substance.

In chapter 5, I will discuss in detail what I call "The elements of worship." I will explain what I believe is imperative in worship; in order to meet God's standard for responding to our burnt offering the way He did with Noah and others.

SENSITIVITY AND HUMILITY

Once again, we need to remain sensitive during the worship encounter for insight, just as Abraham did, regarding the specific mountain in question.

Had he missed the mountain on which to sacrifice his son, like Cain, his sacrifice could have been rejected.

After all, God had demonstrated once with Cain's offering, how important it was that unless we strictly followed His orders, He would not necessarily receive our sacrifices.

Remember Cain's offering was rejected because he did not follow God's instruction to bring an animal instead of foodstuff.

Secondly, under the New Testament, we do not build altars on mountains to offer worship to God. However, for our sacrifice to be satisfactory to God, we need to offer it in a manner that passes the litmus test of God's acceptability.

The patriarch David gives us a hint on how to pass the test, when he pleaded with God in humility and sincerity as he prayed with these words: "Let the words of my mouth and the meditation of my heart be acceptable in your sight, O Lord, my rock and my redeemer." - Psalm 19:14

Clearly, David approached God with humility and not overconfidence. He knew there was a distinct possibility that for whatever reason—possibly his flaws—the words of his mouth and the meditations of his heart could be rejected by God.

Therefore, I submit humility as the other virtue absolutely needed when we come into His presence, to offer sacrifices unto God.

THE UNPREDICTABILITY OF WORSHIP

Abraham did not have full knowledge of everything that was to unfold that fateful morning as he arrived at Moriah. He was strong in faith, knowing that God was able to deliver him from every peril; so must we be trusting of God, especially in the worship experience.

When we come before God to offer up our sacrifice, we should always bear in mind the unpredictability of God, which necessitates the need to be sensitive to the leading of the spirit of God.

We should never come into the worship experience with a pre-conceived notion, or engage the process perfunctorily. Rather we should be buoyant, excited, involved, and expectant; yet remain sensitive to the leading of the Spirit.

There have been numerous times when during our special evening worship service known as the (Evening Sacrifice), the Holy Spirit has prompted me to take the service in a particular direction, not pre-planned.

Sometimes, I have been led to minister directly to certain individuals in a specific way that has led to their healing and deliverance.

We have witnessed marriages strengthened, sick people healed and broken family ties restored as a result of sensitivity to the Holy Spirit during the worship encounter.

LESSON:

God's instruction to Abraham to offer Isaac as a burnt offering on one of the mountains seemed heartlessness.

As though sacrificing his only son was not gruesome and hurtful enough, God seemed to have the audacity to keep Abraham in suspense regarding the location of the 'carnage.'

He therefore had to have heightened sensitivity regarding instructions on the exact site of the sacrifice, if his offering were to be acceptable to God.

As New Testament believers, our *Ultimate Sacrifice* cannot be offered with poor sensitivity, or done superficially. God has demonstrated that He operates in progressive revelation.

Therefore, it behooves the believer, not to operate a mundane routine in worship, but to keep our sensitivity high.

Chapter 3
PREPARATION IN WORSHIP

"And Abraham rose up early in the morning, and saddled his ass, and took two of his young men with him, and Isaac his son, and clave the wood for the burnt offering, and rose up, and went unto the place of which God had told him." - (Genesis 22:3)

In this chapter, we will discuss Abraham's actions or reaction following God's command to bring Isaac to Moriah—to sacrifice him as a burnt offering.

The record will show that everything Abraham did exemplified preparation. You also get a clear sense of his work ethic, even if you have never read about this patriarch until now.

Normally, when people have to go someplace of great importance such as a job interview, or on a first date, or closing a business deal, not only do they have a heightened sense of anxiety, they go through great lengths to prepare.

A befitting definition of preparation is the action or process of making something ready for use or service or of getting ready for some occasion, test, or duty.[13] Abraham took God's orders very seriously as he began to prepare to carry out the task at hand; although a daunting one.

ROSE UP EARLY IN THE MORNING

Early in the morning, Abraham arose in preparation for the pilgrimage to Moriah; a depiction of his absolute commitment to God's instructions to go sacrifice his only son. The scripture says,
"Oh Lord you are my God, early will I seek thee…"
– Psalm 63:1a

There is something to be said about seeking God early; could be early in the morning, or in the early stages of our lives.

Either way, it implies giving God the very best part of our day or life.

We cannot afford to give God our leftovers in true worship, or "look for God" only when we are in trouble.

This is what I call "the spare-tire mentality". It simply means; starting out some kind of project or mission on our own without consulting with God; but

---

[13] htpps://www.merriam-webster.com/dictionary/preparation
© Merriam-Webster Incorporated

running back to Him when we are in trouble or are in need of help.

God, who is rich in mercies, may extend the help we need, but the prudent thing to do is to seek him early or to seek him first.

If you find yourself as a habitual late comer to the House of Worship, there is something gravely wrong with that picture.

If you had a job, I guarantee you would not constantly show up late. We could all learn from the patriarch Abraham, who exemplified how to take our worship life so seriously.

We should plan ahead in arriving at the place of worship on time, not making any excuses for lateness. It is critically important therefore to understand that, to encounter God in true worship, our preparation must precede our praise.

SADDLED HIS DONKEY

Next, Abraham saddled his donkey. A saddle is a seat for the rider of a horse or donkey. To "saddle-up" is to prepare one's horse for riding by putting a saddle on it.[14] It also is the act of climbing into one's ride.

Since the donkey was Abraham's mode of transportation to the place of encounter with God, he took the time to ensure that there would be no problem with his means of transportation.

I would argue that, since in this day and age we do not ride donkeys but drive cars, we take the time to ensure that our mode of transportation to the House of Worship is intact and without incident. This is a portrayal of a man with good work ethic, who wants no excuse for his failure to attend.

As a pastor, I have heard various excuses for failure to attend corporate worship services such as; my car wouldn't start, I have no means of transportation to church, or I have no money for gas to the place of worship.

The shocking thing though is these individuals seem to find a way to get to work from Monday through Friday, or whatever their schedule is, without any difficulty.

---

[14] http://idioms.thefreedictionary.com/saddle+up Copyright © 2003-2017 Farlex, Inc

Ultimate Sacrifice — Joe Kwapong

I quite understand that some people may need assistance in getting to the place of worship, but it becomes a problem when that is the constant excuse, without putting in any effort to rectify the situation.

How come that they find a way to get to work, but seem to find all the excuses when it comes to getting to the place of worship?

Remember, the effort to get to the place of worship was a part of the total sacrifice or the price Abraham had to pay in being obedient to God.

TOOK TWO OF HIS YOUNG MEN

Another interesting lesson here is that; as Abraham prepared to go to the place of worship, he took two of the young men with him.

By implication, Abraham did not go to the House of Worship alone; instead, he brought members of his household with him.

As much as Abraham's motive for travelling with the two young men may have been because they were menservants, the lesson here is that; as priests called to offer sacrifices in the place of worship, we are also to bring people into the House of Worship with us.

Ultimate Sacrifice   Joe Kwapong

We have a mandate from heaven, that starting with members of our own household, we evangelize and disciple them.

Remember in the great commission, Jesus' disciples were to be witnesses starting from their hometown of Jerusalem, then Judea, then to Samaria, then advance to the outermost parts of the world. That was the game-plan.

In my years serving as a pastor, I have seen people who live alone, drive alone, work alone, and so carry the same mentality of being alone into the church. Yes, they do show up in church, but they do so alone because of this mind-set.

This kind of outlook must change, as we should never go to the House of Worship alone. Abraham's example teaches us to be community-oriented rather than being self-centered.

We must endeavor to reach others, a paradigm known as "each one reach one." Every church or believer needs to adapt this mindset of making it a personal conviction to ensure they evangelize and disciple others; a trait Abraham exemplified.

Jesus instructed believers to make disciples of all nations, teaching them to observe all the things He had taught them. A pastor's job is to feed the flock with knowledge and understanding.

I challenge you as a worshiper of God that you always make it a personal responsibility as often as possible, never to go into the House of Worship alone. Determine that the next time you go into the place of worship; you would take other souls with you.

These individuals could be members of your family, community, or co-workers.

THE SACRIFICE

The way Isaac was the sacrifice Abraham was willing to offer as burnt offering is the same way we too must be willing to give up our most-valued treasure, time and talent. Isaac's value is reflected in Abraham and Sarah's estimation of their child, which you would agree was priceless.

Remember, other than loving their son to death, and waiting nearly twenty-five years before giving birth to this 'golden child', they probably were the scorn of their community at some point.

Childlessness in that part of the world, including certain parts of the world today, is frowned upon. How many parents do you know, other than the ones who

Ultimate Sacrifice — Joe Kwapong

stride along now and again with warped mentalities would leave their child unattended with a stranger?

And while that is a rare occurrence, Abraham was willing to give up his son to this invisible Hebrew God. The Scripture says,

"Yet he (Abraham) did not waver through unbelief regarding the promise of God, but was strengthened in his faith and gave glory to God, being fully persuaded that God had power to do what he had promised. - Romans 4:20 & 21 (NIV)

No wonder he was able to exercise faith in trusting God, and offering the one thing that nothing else could replace. God promised him that all of humankind would be blessed through him. What a way to trust God, knowing that this kind of behavior is rewarding.

There are times when it is obvious that, some people show up at the place of worship without their Isaac—their ultimate sacrifice.

They seem to have some kind of sacrifice, but certainly not their Isaac. Remember your Isaac is your most-prized possession; which is your time, your treasure and your talent.

Our sacrifice has to be more than lip-service, as your lips can praise, yet your heart, far, far away—completely detached or absent.

Ultimate Sacrifice   Joe Kwapong

Some people show up at the place of worship for various reasons. Some do out of a sense of obligation, some show up to socialize or catch up with the latest gossip, while others may show up to show off their new clothes or shoes.

There are also those who show up because they genuinely are there to participate, and to offer up true worship. Any genuine sacrifice to God is costly.

It involves and requires the altruistic wholehearted giving away of yourself to God. Your sacrifice of worship is expressed through your time, talent, and your treasure, all of which should be of great value to you.

As worshipers, we should never come into the place of worship without bringing our Isaac. Your Isaac again, is your priced possession. A heartfelt sacrifice is as a sweet-smelling savor in God's nostrils. God appreciates and responds to it, whether in the case of Abel's or Noah's.

The Bible says,
"And the king said unto Araunah, Nay; but I will surely buy it of thee at a price: neither will I offer burnt offerings unto the Lord my God of that which doth cost me nothing; so David bought the threshing floor and

the oxen for fifty shekels of silver." - 2 Samuel 24:24

Sometimes, some people's excuse for not offering their Isaac is that the music was not good enough. They depend on the choir and the band to provide them with a reason to worship.

Clearly, people who do so, lack an understanding of their responsibility in the worship experience. When Abraham went to the place of worship, not only did he prepare himself for the place of worship, he also brought Isaac, his most-treasured possession.

Regardless of what is going on around them, people must come to the place of worship with their Isaac to offer up their best sacrifice to God.

THE WOOD

The Scripture says Abraham "clave the wood for the burnt offering." Therefore the wood was for the burnt offering. In chapter 5, I will discuss the wood in great detail.

By brief introduction, the wood is the element that ensures the fire does not go out, keeping the flame ablaze.

If there was not enough wood, the sacrifice would not be thoroughly consumed. Therefore, it was necessary to ensure there was enough wood on the altar, to keep the fire kindled.

God instructed that,
"The fire shall burn continually upon the altar and not go out.". - Leviticus 6:13

A heart of worship could serve as the wood on the altar of sacrifice. As mentioned earlier, we must always come to the place of worship with a heart ready to be ignited by the fire of the Holy Spirit. We will also discuss, in-depth, what the wood symbolizes.

ROSE UP AND WENT

It is interesting that the scripture takes notice of the fact that Abraham actually "rose up and went to the place of worship." The fact that he did that, tells me that Abraham was everything but a procrastinator, who would find all the excuses not to participate in worship.

We see a man poised, ready to go to the place of worship no matter what. Whether we are engaged in personal or corporate worship, it is imperative to have this posture.

Our worship to God must come from a place of poise and of willingness, gratitude and brokenness, to engage God's manifest presence.

Just as Abraham rose up and went, out of a sense of wanting to connect with God, rather than one of coercion, the true worship encounter comes from a place of willingness to engage.

The same principle applies when it comes to our giving of money. We should not allow ourselves to be pressured by others to give. Rather, it should be a personal decision.

The Scripture declares that,
"Every man according as he purposes in his heart so let him give; not grudgingly or of necessity, for God loves a cheerful giver." – 2 Corinthians 9:7

WENT UNTO THE PLACE

The lesson here is that finally, Abraham actually made his way to the place where God had instructed him about.

Although without great details, this remarkable man actually took steps of faith that etched him closer and closer to his destination.

This phenomenon is what I call taking baby steps into your destiny. In life, we may not have all the answers, but we certainly know enough to inspire us to take these baby steps.

Lao Tzu is quoted as saying: *"The journey of a thousand miles begins with a single step."*

Therefore, with God's help, we must endeavor to take the first steps. Go back and get that high-school diploma. Register that new business, clean up your credit, or make plans to buy your next home.

Take that step of faith, and before you know it, you will be taking territories. You may start off at cruise control, but you will move into overdrive in Jesus name!

Remember, if you can make it to the holy mountain of God in worship, there is healing, deliverance, refreshing, joy, restoration, promotion and many more blessings than you can handle.

PRAYER:

Father, I thank you for the opportunity to join other believers in Christ to corporately worship you, and I also thank you that you hear my voice and prayer as an individual.

Today, I come to you in the name of Jesus, and ask that you please help prepare me as a vessel, ready for the Master's use.

Ultimate Sacrifice — Joe Kwapong

Like the patriarch Abraham, please prepare me. Like Moses, grant me a mountain-top experience today and, like Elijah, let the fire burn within my soul.

Chapter 4
GOING DEEPER IN WORSHIP

"Then on the third day Abraham lifted up his eyes, and saw the place afar off. And Abraham said unto his young men, abide ye here with the ass and I and the lad will go yonder and worship, and come again to you." - Genesis 22:4-5.

After three days of embarking on a search for the holy mountain upon which to bring God his ultimate sacrifice, Abraham lifted up his eyes, and finally could perceive the place from a distance.

According to biblical numerology, the number three signifies *completion or perfection, and unity.* Three is the number of Persons in the Trinity.

Many significant events in the Bible happened on the third day. The scripture tells us that,
"After two days he will revive us; on the third day he will restore us that we may live in his presence." - Hosea 6:2

Jonah spent three days and three nights in the belly of the fish; according to Matthew 12:40, after which—when he had had the time to clearly think through carrying out God's order to preach in the city of Nineveh, rather than his initial blatant disregard—the fish vomited Jonah at shore, giving him a new lease on life!

According to Luke 13:7, not only did Jesus' earthly ministry last for three years, He was raised back from the grave on the third day, after being dead and buried.

Therefore, *"the third day"* phenomenon refers to a time of resurrection, new lease on life, and great possibilities!

A time when confusion, perplexity, anxiety, and uncertainty, all come to an end! For Abraham to finally discern the mountain upon which to sacrifice Isaac, and to engage this Hebrew God on His terms, he needed to be sensitive to His leading.

As New Testament believers, we ought to be sensitive to God and the leadings of the Holy Spirit during the time of worship.

It should not be taken lightly. I have seen some phenomenal things take place when everyone is attuned and sensitive to the Holy Spirit during times of worship.

Anything impossible with humankind is possible during such times. Therefore, whenever we engage God in true worship, He will always cause us to experience a "third-day" phenomenon, just like He allowed Abraham to do.

I also call the "third-day" phenomenon, *"Times of Refreshing from the presence of the Lord."*

The scripture says,

"Repent ye therefore, and be converted, that your sins may be blotted out, when the times of refreshing shall come from the presence of the Lord." - Acts 10:19.

Besides being anxious and not having full disclosure of his pilgrimage, Abraham obeyed God and took a step of faith in following God's direction and experienced "the third-day" phenomenon.

God's presence was made known to Abraham. The "third-day" experience will be a day of restoration and completion or perfection.

PROPHETIC DECREE:

You may be going through a tough time right now. Probably a financial challenge, not knowing how you are going to get out of a college loan, or pay your mortgage, or provide for your family. I sense and decree a major breakthrough is coming your way, right now! In Jesus' Name!

In fact, if you would dare to give God your Isaac—your best effort or even your brokenness—He will cause a complete turnaround in your situation, right now.

Your struggle is over! Your dark days are gone! I see the breaking of dawn. Everything is taking a turn for the better, in Jesus' mighty name! There is hope yet, so don't give up; not now, not ever!

ABIDE HERE

Next, Abraham instructed the two young men he had brought with him to Moriah, to *"abide here"* with the donkey while he went yonder to worship and return to them.

As I mentioned in chapter 3, as much as we can only speculate Abraham's motive for travelling with the two young men to Moriah, we can categorically state that these were menservants who served and kept his estate.

Therefore, although they may have been travelling on assignment as servants on their master's pilgrimage, Abraham nonetheless had brought members of his household to the place of worship.

This I would argue is a sign of stewardship, taking some responsibility for bringing people into the House of Worship.

To buttress this point, we are told in the scriptures of how God, before destroying Sodom and Gomorrah, revealed His intentions to Abraham. This was because; Abraham was to be a great nation through whom other nations were going to be blessed and; also, God trusted Abraham to teach and train his children and *"the sons of his household to keep the way of the Lord and to do what was right and just".* – (Genesis 18:19)

It is not surprising therefore, that Abraham had brought those two men with him to the place of worship.

PART OF YOUR WORSHIP

Even if Abraham may have brought these two for the wrong reason; they were at the 'House of Worship' nonetheless.

We may not have all been called as pastors and great evangelists such as Billy Graham, but as part of our ultimate sacrifice, we have all been given the task or assignment to evangelize and disciple the lost.

Therefore, the mandate to seek out and to bring the lost to the House of Worship, even if it was done improperly is a big part of our ultimate sacrifice.

The apostle Paul also argued this position when he said; "some indeed preach Christ even out of envy and strife," and even though those people preached Christ *"out of contention, not sincerely... Christ is preached;* he argued, and *"I therein do rejoice."*

Furthermore, the eagled-eye prophet declares;
"It shall come to pass in the last days, that the mountain of the LORD's house shall be established on the top of the mountains, and shall be exalted above the hills; and all nations shall flow unto it." – Isaiah 2:2

ABIDE HERE WHILE I GO YONDER

This statement underscores the fact that to attain certain heights in life, a certain level of self-imposed solitary confinement or separation—not asking every Tom, Dick, and Harry to tag along with us—is required.

Naturally, we are wired not to be alone, and to underscore that fact, God affirmed this when He said; "It is not good for the man to be alone." – Genesis 2:18a

As a result of this, the natural recourse is to travel in a pack, or not to go it alone. Again, whereas the *"community"* mentality is intrinsic and rewarding, certain heights in life can only be attained when we break away from the pack, to be alone with the Creator of the universe, in true worship.

GOING DEEPER IN WORSHIP

Abraham then said "I and the lad will go yonder and worship." This is what I refer to as; "going deeper in worship."

If anyone was going to be left at the periphery it was neither going to be Abraham nor his son. I strongly believe going deeper in worship is a choice.

It never ceases to amaze me how Abraham and members of his household came into Moriah to worship, yet it was him and Isaac alone who went "a little farther to worship."

There are instances both in the scriptures and in my ministry, where there has been abundance of God's provision through His manifest presence, yet some get to receive of Him while others remain spectators.

The key is that Abraham demonstrated that he wanted more, and that he wanted to go deeper into the mountain of worship, and that makes all the difference between God revealing Himself and Him not showing up.

While the scripture admonishes us to
"Seek the LORD while He may be found; Call upon Him while He is near," – Isaiah 55:6
It also says;
"God rewards those who earnestly and diligently seek Him." – Hebrews 11:6b

I have seen people who are inattentive and distracted during the time of corporate worship, yet they expect God to miraculously touch them, and provide all their needs.

True worship requires that we push a little farther and dig a little deeper, until there is a true encounter with Divinity.

SHUT OUT THE NOISE

Going deeper also means; "shutting out the noise or the distraction." Anything that shifts the focus off God, and stifles the building of an atmosphere that helps worshippers stay focused on Him, must be removed.

Such distractive elements include disorder, disunity, dysfunction, disruption; just to name a few. In Chapter 12, I will discuss into detail, some of these elements, and how to minimize them in order to optimize your worship encounter.

Growing up as a young boy in the traditional church I attended, whenever congregants arrived late while corporate worship was in session, they were prevented from distracting the service, and made to wait outside the sanctuary until such a time that it was practical to join the rest of the congregation. This was the church's way of keeping order.

Shutting out the noise could also mean coming to the place where everyone's focus is on this Holy God and Him only. It is a place you come to where you empty yourself of all the chaos and distractions going on in your life and concentrating all of your energies on the Most-High God. Under such conditions, worship will be an intimate experience between you and God.

I WILL COME AGAIN TO YOU

Finally, Abraham's profound words to the young men were; "I will come again, to you."

How was he so sure that he would return to them? Did he even have a clue whether, like his child, he too could lose his life?

What if Isaac fought back? For me that statement was so prophetic; and the interpretation of what was impressed upon my heart was that, whenever we come into the place of true worship, we are most certainly guaranteed a return.

Better than an astute investor who looks for a guaranteed return on a good investment, there is an assurance of a transformation as a result of engaging God's presence in the worship experience.

Going in confused but coming out enlightened, sick but coming out healed, dispirited but coming out consoled, refreshed, and rejuvenated! I can totally understand Abraham saying 'I will return.'

PROPHETIC DECREE

Beloved, as you read this book, I prophesy to you by the Lord that regardless of whatever condition you may find yourself in, you will engage the Hand of God in true worship; that will cause you to come out of your situation.

Like Abraham I say to you; you will return, better than where you used to be, into the place of God's very best for your life!

I speak to every barrenness, drug addiction, old habits, family yokes and curses to be broken and destroyed in Jesus' mighty name. Amen!

I declare and decree that you are coming out of every situation that has held you captive, rendered you ineffective, and that no weapon formed against you will prosper in Jesus' name. Amen!

Chapter 5

SETTING THE STAGE FOR WORSHIP

"And Abraham took the wood of the burnt offering and laid it upon Isaac his son; and he took the fire in his hand, a knife; and they went both of them together." - (Genesis 22:6)

Although not authoritatively stated, we get a sense that Abraham had finally located the very mountain upon which God had wanted Isaac sacrificed.

The text indicates that he hardly wasted any time in proceeding to set the stage to begin offering his *Ultimate Sacrifice*—his only son Isaac.

Like Christ, Isaac epitomized God's only son whom He sent to Calvary, to die for the sins of humankind.

"He was oppressed, yet when he was afflicted he opened not his mouth; as a lamb that is led to the slaughter, and as a sheep that before their shearer is dumb, so he opened not his mouth." --Isaiah 53:7

I can only imagine the trauma of being faced with the dilemma of carrying out a divine order to sacrifice your son. Yet, this seemed to be in conflict with natural law; an act tantamount to a barbaric act of murder, punishable either by life in imprisonment or capital punishment.

Furthermore, I thought about the impossible task of carefully explaining to his wife Sarah why sacrificing their only son, whom they had waited for nearly twenty-five years to give birth to, could possibly be justifiable.

Would Sarah think her husband was being delusional? Or even possibly having early symptoms of dementia? Was God going to intervene at some point, or was He going to stand aloof and watch a father painfully lose his son?

ABraham must have had a lot going on in his mind. Did God really ask him to kill his only son? Could it have been his imagination? How many times do we get to this point in our own lives?

PROPHETIC DECLARATION

I would like to come into a prayer of agreement with you right now, to speak over you that whatever you may have lost—whether it was a child, a sibling, a mother or father, a wife or husband, a loved-one, a marriage, or some property you worked all your adult life for—but thought God stood by and watched you suffer that loss, without intervening, will turn around bringing you restoration, restitution and reconciliation now in Jesus' name!

You will recover every loss! Your health will be restored, your marriage will be healed, and your family will be preserved, delivered, and strengthened, in Jesus' name!

There is hope yet, so don't give up, and don't give in. I see things turning around for the better! I declare a season of change and hope. You will recover everything you have lost, in Jesus name, amen!

THE FIVE ELEMENTS OF TRUE WORSHIP

The 5 elements of worship were absolutely necessary, if Abraham was going to carry out God's order to get into the land of Moriah to offer his only son Isaac as a burnt offering.

These "elements" are symbolic of certain divinely-instituted ordinances, which necessitate the true worship encounter.

I have been greatly troubled by some people who over emphasize certain ordinances as having greater significance over others. In my view, this is erroneous and imbalanced.

THE WOOD

In Chapter 3, I made a brief reference to the wood which Abraham brought along to the place of worship.

At this point, I will share with you into greater detail, what I believe the wood symbolizes. Please bear in mind that, this is only my view on the subject, and does not in any way, claim mastery or monopoly of the interpretation of what holy men inspired by God, wrote.

The wood symbolizes a myriad of things. By simple logic, once it was ignited, the wood was the "fuel" that kept the fire going.

Therefore, I would argue that the wood is symbolic of **divinely-instituted ordinances** that create the atmosphere for the believer to engage the manifest presence of God. Some of these are:

THE CROSS

First, the wood is symbolic of the Cross on which Christ was crucified. Quoted about fifty-four times in the New Testament and known as the Messianic prophet, Isaiah prophesied about the coming of Christ, more than any other Old Testament prophet.

In addition, he is the only prophet to have given a vivid description of the crucifixion of Christ. Writing under the theme Salvation through the Messiah—the servant of the Lord—the eagle-eyed prophet gave a graphic description of the death of Christ in Isaiah 52:13 through 53:12.

Therefore, the wood reminds the New Testament believer that, like Christ, the *Ultimate Sacrifice* is a life *"crucified with Christ"*- nevertheless *"I live; yet not I, but Christ lives through me."*

PRAYER

The first words of Jesus, when He introduced us to the Church were that His house would be known as *"the house of prayer for all nations."*

Again, in Luke's Gospel chapter 18:1, it is written; *"Men always are to pray and not to faint,"* making the unequivocal argument that it is imperative to constantly pray as believers.

The constant offering of prayer, has a direct bearing on the consistent burning of the wood that ensured the sacrifice would burn all the way through. If there was not ample wood, the sacrifice would not be thoroughly consumed.

Therefore, so the fire would never go out, it was apposite to ensure there was enough wood on the altar. In the scriptures, God instructed that,
"The fire shall burn continually upon the altar and not go out."- Leviticus 6:13.

THE LORD'S SUPPER

Another divine ordinance that sets the atmosphere for a divine encounter is "the Lord's Supper," known in the Old Testament as The Passover.

During the time of its institution, it was to begin on the 15th day of the Hebrew month Nisan, which typically falls in March or April of the Gregorian calendar.

God's order to Moses was that, depending on the size of a household, each house would provide a male sheep or goat without blemish on the first day of the month Nisan.

Afterwards, the entire population was to kill the animal, the night of the 14th of that same month. They would then take the blood and smear it on the two side posts and the upper door of their house.

The animal would then be eaten at night, roasted with fire, unleavened bread and bitter herbs.

God instructed that this and other ordinances be kept as a feast for generations to come. (Exodus 12:14)

When the apostle Paul wrote about this in the New Testament, he made the same salient point that as often as Christians partook of this sacred ordinance—eating of the bread that symbolizes the broken body of Christ, and drinking of the wine; which is symbolic of the new covenant—Christians were proclaiming the death, burial, and resurrection of Christ until His return.

This, the apostle argues, is an eternal ordinance that proclaims the death, burial, and resurrection of Christ. - (1 Corinthians 11:23-26).

GIVING OF ALMS

Another ordinance is the giving of alms or showing mercy to widows, orphans, and the poor. In the story of the rich, young ruler who came to Jesus, the discourse was about the way to salvation or eternal life. (Matthew 19:16–22)

Jesus, in answering him, shockingly recommended to this young man who had great possessions to; *"go sell"* his belongings and *"give it to the poor."* That way, Jesus said; he would *"have treasure stored up in heaven."*

One singular, earthly act of kindness to the poor was going to produce a guaranteed eternal and heavenly reward.

Quintessentially, the young man went away with great sorrow because the Scripture says "*he had great possessions.*"

THE SACRIFICE---YOUR ISAAC

The next element Abraham needed to have present for his sacrifice was Isaac. Giving God your Isaac simply means sacrificing your very best, and not your leftovers.

As we have clearly seen, Abraham and his wife Sarah had to wait for nearly twenty-five years before giving birth to their only son Isaac.

Abraham demonstrates that without reservation or hesitation, he was willing to give up Isaac as a sacrifice to God.

Therefore, to give God our Isaac is to give him our very best; that which we hold so near and dear to our hearts. Such things as our time, talents, and anything else we treasure.

To give God our Isaac means not holding back our very best from God. As the Church is the embodiment of Christ on earth, we give to the mission of the Church.

The Church goes out into the marketplace, and represents Christ. Whenever or whatever you give to the Church, I believe, should be your responsibility to ensure that you are giving to a worthy cause.

A place that has a track record of actually doing something in the community that is tangible and can be verified.

Because your Isaac is of such high value, you have a responsibility to follow God's strict orders in this offering. You have to make sure that the elements are in place before laying your Isaac upon the altar of sacrifice.

THE FIRE

Next, the scripture says Abraham *"took the fire in his hand."* Obviously, fire was significant to ensuring that the Ultimate Sacrifice was burnt.

Remember God had instructed that the fire had to be kept burning on the altar continually, and not go out. (Leviticus 6:13)

Ultimate Sacrifice   Joe Kwapong

When the prophet Elijah threw down the gauntlet with the prophets of Baal on Mount Carmel, the *"fire of the Lord fell"* after he had prayed to the God of Abraham, Isaac and Israel, affirming Yahweh as the only true God, and Elijah as His spokesman.

When God spoke from the burning bush to Moses, which was a manifestation of God Himself, Moses turned away from the sight *"because he was afraid to look at God."* - Exodus 3:7

Also we are told that
"Mount Sinai was covered with smoke, because the Lord descended on it in fire. The smoke billowed up from it like smoke from a furnace, and the whole mountain trembled violently." – Exodus 19:16 (NIV).

Again, the scripture declares,
"To the Israelites the glory of the Lord looked like a consuming fire on top of the mountain."- Exodus 24:17 (NIV).

In the account of the Apostle John's vision of Christ in the book of Revelations, he describes Him as having *"eyes like a blazing fire."* – (Revelation 1:14c).

The Apostle Paul also describes the second coming of Christ as coming *"in blazing fire". (*2 Thessalonians 1:8).

Again, the scripture states,
"For our God is a consuming fire." - Hebrews 12:29
Therefore, akin to the Old Testament depiction of fire is the New.

Evidently, fire was the manifestation and approval of God for the burnt offering! In the New Testament church, where we live in the dispensation of the Holy Spirit and of grace, our "worship" is worthless without the approval and involvement of the Holy Spirit, as His fire purges us.

STRANGE FIRE

Nadab and Abihu, the sons of Aaron, took censers, put fire in them, placed incense on it, and offered *strange fire* before the Lord, which He had not commanded them to do. As a result, fire came out from the presence of the Lord and devoured them, and they died before the Lord. (Leviticus 10:1-2)

On other occasions, the Lord had received incense from the priests; therefore, this incident seemed out of character for God not only to reject Nadab and Abihu's sacrifice but also to kill them.

Why would a well-intended act attract such a fatal reprimand? A close study of Moses' response to his grieving brother Aaron revealed the reason.

"Then Moses said to Aaron, it is what the Lord spoke, saying, 'By those who come near me I will be treated as holy, and before all the people I will be honored. So Aaron, therefore, kept silent." –Leviticus 10:3 (NAS 1977)

You offer strange fire when you approach and treat godly things in an unholy manner, and fail to honor Him before the people.

THE KNIFE

Before the animal being sacrificed was placed on the altar and burnt, it first had to be killed. The knife was the tool for killing the animal. As a result, the knife was symbolic of the painful experiences we go through that result in dying to self, not as a result of wrongdoing, but as true-disciples of Christ.

When an animal is killed, blood is spilt. The Scripture declares,

"For the life of the flesh is in the blood: and I have given it to you upon the altar to make atonement for your souls: for it is the blood that makes atonement for the soul." (Leviticus 11:1-2)

Every sacrifice therefore, required blood, which represents life. Remember; "without the shedding of blood, there is no forgiveness of sins."

Therefore, the knife reminds us of:

- The self-denial and shameful death our Lord and Savior Jesus Christ exemplified, as He bled for humankind on Calvary's Cross.
- Apostles Paul and Barnabas who suffered the fiery furnace of affliction including being nearly stoned to death, remembering that;

"We must go through many tribulations and hardships to enter the kingdom of God." - Acts 1422b

- The fact that when we experience the new birth, our old sinful Adamic nature is dead to sin, and alive to Christ. Therefore, living the devout life of a Christian—who must learn to *"die daily"*—means giving up old habits which die slowly and painfully.

The Ultimate Sacrifice goes beyond melodic harmonies, perfect pitch and skillful music. It involves dying to self, and being prepared to lay down our lives in defense of the gospel.

THE ALTAR

In Chapter 7, we will discuss the significance of the altar as well as its relevance in modern-day Christian life. What I will do here is to share a brief historical background of ancient altars, which were structures commonly found at shrines, temples and other places of worship.

In the ancient world, altars were raised platforms or structures usually made of dirt, stones, carved rocks, or elaborate articles of furniture, [15] upon which sacrifices were made for religious purposes.

The Hebrew word *"mizbeach"* translated as *"altar"* means *"a place of slaughter."*[16] Also known in the Greek as *"bomos,"* "altar" means *"an elevated place,"* on which to offer sacrifice.[17]

Places where altars were built were considered holy and sacred. Often times there were angelic sightings or encounters at the sites of altars.

---

[15] www.bible-history.com/sketches/ancient/ancient-altars.html
©Bible History Online.
[16] www.biblehub.com/Hebrew/4196.htm
Strong's/NAS Exhaustive Concordance ©1981, 1998 by The Lockman Foundation.
[17] www.classic.studylight.org/lex/grk/view.cgi?number=1041
Thayer and Smith. "The New Testament Greek Lexicon."

To reiterate this point, altars were mostly for sacrificing, but other times they were built as a memorial, as the one built by Moses and named Jehovah Nissi.

Remember, as New Testament Christians, we have to build lasting altars for sacrifice. An altar of sacrifice is not only limited to prayer; instead, it includes your devotional life.

The Bible says,
"Oh God, thou art my God; early will I seek thee: my soul thirst for thee, my flesh longs for thee in a dry and thirsty land, where no water is." Psalm 63:1.

Remember, having a devotional life where the fire on the altar never ceases is part of our reasonable service to God.

WENT WITH HIS SACRIFICE

I was so fascinated by the fact that Abraham and his son Isaac *"both went together..."* to the mountain of the Lord.

Considering Isaac as the Ultimate Sacrifice, Abraham went attached to his sacrifice—a costly, carefully—prepared sacrifice.

This is a very important principle in the worship encounter, as there have been countless times when I have attended worship services, and seen laity and leadership; pastors and parishioners alike, who come into the worship experience empty-handed—unattached to any sacrifice.

In some instances, these have been the keynote speakers, who are required to know better. Instead of actively participating in the corporate worship, they expect the congregants to be docile, eager to welcome a star-studded, celebrity preacher.

You would be absolutely right if you guessed that *"with them, the Lord was not pleased."*

Instead of that kind of hawkish attitude, God expects all of His children to humbly come attached to their sacrifice, whenever we come to the mountain of the Lord to worship.

Other times, it has been parishioners who, unlike Abraham, failed to rise early to adequately prepare their ultimate sacrifice before arriving at the mountain of the Lord for the worship encounter.

Everything is done so haphazardly and there is no fire to ignite the sacrifice. Everything is mundane and heartless.

The smoke of the burnt offering does not rise to the nostrils of God, because there is no sacrifice on the altar.

Chapter 6
FATHER AND SON IN WORSHIP

"And Isaac spoke unto Abraham his father, and said, my father: and he said; here am I, my son. And he said behold the fire and the wood: but where is the lamb for a burnt offering? And Abraham said, my son, God will provide himself a lamb for a burnt offering: so they went both of them together". - *(*Genesis 22:7-8)

The dialogue between Abraham and his son Isaac is by far one of the most riveting parts of the entire story.

We can position ourselves there to eavesdrop on what could well have been an emotional conversation between a father who was about to kill and offer his son to God as a burnt offering—an innocent son who blindly followed his father like the proverbial lamb led to the slaughter.

Yet, he had to constrain himself from being overly emotional; trusting that by some supernatural intervention, his son's life would be spared.

Isaac calls out to his father as though he needed the reassurance of his father's presence at the place of worship.

"My father," he says. His father, sensing a cocktail of desperation and uncertainty in his son's voice, and mixed perhaps with his own emotions, answers; "Here I am my son;" as if to say we are in this together, my son! I have not abandoned you, nor do I intend to do so.

PROPHET AND PRIEST

Abraham exemplifies a very compelling principle. As fathers, not only are we Progenitors, but part of our God-given, innate function is also to operate as Priest, Prophet, Provider and Protector of the family.

A prophet hears messages from God and communicates it to the people; whereas a priest communicates the petition of the people to God.

Secondly, by being physically present at the mountain of the Lord with his son to offer his *Ultimate Sacrifice*, Abraham was teaching us the invaluable need as parents, to demonstrate firsthand to our children, the importance of taking seriously, our place as priests of our home.

Instead of simply telling Isaac to go to church, be a good child, pay attention to his teachers, do what is right etc., Abraham actually exemplified his priestly role

In addition, Abraham was to illustrate the execution of the priestly office to his son. That way, not only would he teach his son the traditions of the priesthood, he would also ensure his son would continue in the traditions of the priesthood, as God had instructed Abraham. God vouched for Abraham to keep the tradition by saying,

"For I know him, that he will command his children and his household after him, and they shall keep the way of the LORD, to do justice and judgment; that the LORD may bring upon Abraham that which he hath spoken of him." - (Genesis 18:19).

ALARMING STATISTICS

As a husband and father, it breaks my heart—and I believe the ultimate Father's heart as well—to see the absentee-father crisis or the lack of father-figures mentoring the younger generation in our society.

There is such a decline; the problem is fast becoming an epidemic.

According to US census bureau; 24 million US children (1 out of every 3) live without their birth father. Fatherless boys and girls are two times as likely to drop out of high school, two times as likely to end up in jail, and four times more likely to need help for emotional or behavioral problems.

The census further reveals, 90% of homeless and runaway children are from fatherless homes, while 80% of rapists motivated with displaced anger come from fatherless homes.[18]

Anybody looking at these statistics must have their stomach turn. The reality is stark; the figures alarming and the truth of needing an intervention cannot be overstretched.

With the absence of fathers, and father-figures, where do we begin to deal with raising a generation of priests and leaders?

The fathers who are supposed to lead by example are missing in action. As a result, children are left to raise children, and to have free rein.

Growing up as a child in the generation X era, we were not perfect by any stretch of the imagination. However, we were raised in a fairly-decent manner

---

[18] www.thefatherlessgeneration.wordpress.com/statistics

that, in comparison, cries for a revival for the millennial generation.

My mother for instance, taught us to always say grace before meals. Respect for the elderly was strictly adhered to; even to the most-rebellious child in the neighborhood, it came as second-nature.

Without good etiquette, following rules, attending church, saying your prayers before going to bed, and did I mention respect for the elderly; we were guaranteed to catch some form of punishment or a beat-down for non-conformance. If you had any questions, you spoke only when you were spoken to.

Not to be confused with a military barracks, we had some good times as well. Though not overtly religious, my father made sure we attended church without fail.

He took pride in being a provider and protector of the family. Ironically, he was also the parent you could pull a fast one on. When he sent you to the shop, the change was yours! I wouldn't trade my dad for all the diamonds in Russia, Canada or the southern African country of Botswana.

WHERE IS THE LAMB FOR SACRIFICE?

Next, no longer able to hide his curiosity, Isaac asked his father a weighty question; one that required deep soul-searching.

As if to say to his father; I may not be an expert, but I sure know something is gravely wrong with this sacred ritual about to go down.

"Behold the fire and wood, but where is the lamb for the burnt offering"? – (Genesis 22:7). He asks.

You have to assume that either Isaac was familiar with the burnt-offering process, or the kid was simply a genius who figured out his daddy needed some steak on the grill.

At least, he could recognize the missing element as the lamb for the burnt offering. The problem is that, there is such a lack of an understanding of spiritual protocol in our generation.

It would make Abraham cringe if he walked our streets today. Although times and the practice have changed, the principles remain unaffected.

In my estimation, part of the reason why there is such a lack of understanding and appreciation for this protocol is due to the failure of fathers and mothers to prepare the next generation to know God in a meaningful way as did Abraham.

WORSHIP WITHOUT A LAMB

By all accounts, a complete physical exam that fails to screen a patient for cholesterol, blood pressure, blood sugar, listening to the heart or lungs can conclusively be classified as *fraudulent*.

Yet, like a visit to the doctor's office, some New Testament believers fail to perform self-examination on the condition of their spiritual health.

First the scripture says,
"Therefore if you bring your gift to the altar, and there remember that your brother has something against you, leave your gift there before the altar, and go your way. First be reconciled to your brother, and then come and offer your gift." Matthew 5:23-24.

Clearly, the recommendation from this scripture is first, to *be reconciled* if there is an offence at the time of sacrifice.

Like the doctor, the parishioner has to perform self-examination to check for abnormalities, then work to administer corrective medication before proceeding with the holy ordinance.

However, the scripture also points out the *gift* that has to be brought to the altar. That gift is what Isaac refers to as *"the lamb"* for the sacrifice.

Over the years, I have seen leaders and laity alike, who attend corporate worship without a lamb for the burnt offering.

They come dressed up, looking and smelling good which they should; yet there is such a lack of preparation for the sacred ritual of offering spiritual sacrifices to God.

Isaac's prophetic question to his father still goes unanswered by the Church today. I see the trappings; but where is the *ultimate sacrifice*?

The 21st century Church has all the modern architecturally-prestigious buildings and stained-glass cathedrals, the philharmonic choirs, strobe lights, smoke-machines, etc., which are all worthy of the tourist-attraction status they have earned.

Yet the real question is; where is our broken and contrite spirit? Where are the qualities which, like the lamb without blemish, make for the *ultimate sacrifice?*

Worship without a lamb for the burnt offering is just like the complete physical exam that ignores all the basic checks—a complete sham!

GOD WILL PROVIDE

When asked where the lamb for the burnt offering was, Abraham's answer was; *"my son God will provide himself a lamb for a burnt offering"*.

By this time, this was Isaac's third question to his dad since he began the interrogation. There are three things that captivate my heart, as I reenact the entire episode in my imagination.

Firstly, I see a father who is carefully and patiently answering a barrage of questions until his perseverance to educate his son about a religious ritual is crowned with success.

Secondly, although his father seemed unperturbed, Abraham must have been battling mixed emotions.

On the one hand, he had to maintain his composure while carefully choosing his words in answering his son - in order not to give away his marching orders to offer his son as a burnt offering.

Then, there is the prophetic answer Abraham gave to his son; *"God will provide Himself a lamb for a burnt offering."*

As if to say; I have limitations, my son. I don't always have the answers or know what to do, but the all-sufficient Heavenly Father always does.

He is the Provider, and will supply what is needed to make this work. Abraham pointed to the ultimate Father as the provider-in-chief, who has no limitations!

Dear reader, I need you to understand that God does not demand anything from us He hasn't already provided us with.

He gave you and I the breath of life; and demands that with the life He gave us, we serve Him. He also gives us the strength to work, and asks that we bring Him a tithe as an act of obedience, in order to multiply our blessing.

He gave Abraham and his wife Sarah, a child; and asked him for a sacrifice He had already provided. God is a giver; not a taker. If you and I can give God the same quality seed Abraham offered, He will provide the same way He did Abraham.

Will you give God your treasure, talent, time, sickness, insecurity or even family?

Remember, God is absolutely pleased when we execute our responsibility to teach and train our children in understanding spiritual protocol.

The manner in which God literally vouched for Abraham was admirable. He declared,

"For I know him, that he will command his children and his household after him, and they shall keep the way of the lord, to do justice and judgment; that the lord may bring upon Abraham that which he hath spoken of him."- Genesis 18:19.

Worship is therefore more than singing melodic or pitch-perfect songs. When we execute our charge to teach and train our children in understanding spiritual protocol, like Abraham did, it is our reasonable service to God, which also constitutes worship.

THEY WENT BOTH TOGETHER

In the last paragraph of the previous chapter you just read, there is a similar subtitle like the one under which I am writing. If you are thinking it was repeated by error, it was not.

Rather, it is a deliberate attempt to use the same scenario to underscore two separate points. Whereas in the previous paragraph Isaac is a metaphor for his father's sacrifice, this paragraph emphasizes the bond between a father and son worshiping together.

Frankly, it is heartbreaking when a father or mother who is supposed to exemplify the worship of the one true God to their children, lacks the willingness or understanding of what it takes to do so themselves. God's idea of maintaining a godly world in which His will is done and His kingdom established, is one that a righteous parent raises their children in the fear and admonition of God.

Abraham was such an exemplary parent who demonstrated to his son everything it takes to offer the *ultimate sacrifice* at the place of worship.

He does not only talk to his son about God, he actually gets involved in serving and worshipping God; making Abraham an active and willing parent who participates in the worship of God.

In the last decade, I have been so burdened with the vision to institute *"father and son in worship;"*

This will be a special community outreach in which males of all race, ethnicity, economic status, creed and political affiliation, gather to mentor the younger generation on how to take their God-given leadership role as protectors of their community and providers of their homes very seriously.

Therefore, I challenge every Christian father, man, uncle, nephew, grandfather, great grandfather, or male pastor, to purposefully mentor a child, especially a male child, teaching them how to execute their God-given role as priests. I believe that would make such a difference in reversing some of the adverse effects of absentee fatherhood.

When His disciples asked Him a question regarding how to pray, Jesus answered by teaching them a prayer model.

When you pray, He said; your prayer must begin by addressing God as your heavenly Father; implying prayer has to be birthed out of a relationship with God.

Now I must admit; there are several people whose earthly fathers may not have done the best job of modeling exemplary fatherhood.

Their only memory of a father was a male who hardly came around, but whenever he did, his visit would be one laced with hostility and criticism.

For such people, relating to a loving heavenly Father is not practical due to the fact that they have yet to experience the true love of a father.

Therefore, the mental depiction of God as a loving father may not sit well with them, due to their bitter experience.

DECLARATION

Heavenly Father, I thank You that You are the Ultimate Father who loves me unconditionally. You demonstrated Your love for me by sending Your only Son; Jesus Christ, to die for me.

Today, I embrace Your love for me, and let go of any hostility, unforgiveness, resentment or bitterness I may have in my heart.

I decree that I am forgiven, delivered, healed, loved, and restored; that I may worship You with a clean heart. I thank You, in Jesus' mighty name, amen!

Chapter 7
BUILDING AN ALTAR OF WORSHIP

"And they came to the place which God had told him of; and Abraham built an altar there, and laid the wood in order, and bound Isaac his son, and laid him on the altar upon the wood." -Genesis 22:9

Finally, Abraham and his son had discovered and arrived at the exact "Mountain of the Lord."

As we follow the trail, it is evident that their destination was discovered through obedience, sensitivity, preparation, perseverance, hard work and faith.

This was the place I call *there*—where the entire encounter with God was to take place. Abraham's next assignment was to build an altar.

The building of the altar was significant to the sacrifice, as without the altar, there would be no authorized place to lay the wood and sacrifice for the burnt offering.

In Chapter 5, I wrote about the 5 elements of worship, which included a brief history of the altar.

However, here, we will discuss the altar in greater detail, as well as its correlation with modern-day Christian life.

Again, in the ancient world, altars were raised platforms or structures usually made of dirt, stones, carved rocks, or elaborate articles of furniture, upon which sacrifices were made for religious purposes.

Again, the Hebrew word *"mizbeach"* translated as *"altar"* means *"a place of slaughter."* Also known in the Greek as *"bomos,"* "altar" means *"an elevated place,"* on which to offer sacrifice.

Places where altars were built were considered holy and sacred. Often times there were angelic sightings or encounters at the sites of altars.

Remember altars were mostly for sacrificing, but other times they were built as a memorial; as the one built by Moses and named Jehovah Nissi.

On the Day of Atonement for instance, a special day of forgiveness for the children of Israel which occurred annually, the High Priest would offer sacrifice on behalf of the people in the outer court on the bronze altar.

The blood of the animal would then be brought into the inner chamber, also known as the Holy Place, then into the Holy of Holies by the High Priest, and sprinkled on the mercy seat. [19]

Although there could have possibly been the involvement of an altar when Abel sacrificed to the Lord in Genesis 4:4, the first mention of an altar was said to have been erected by Noah.

After the flood, we are told that;
"Then Noah built an altar to the Lord, he took some of every kind of clean animal and every kind of clean bird and offered burnt offerings on the altar.   When the Lord smelled the pleasing aroma, He said to Himself, "I will never again curse because of man, even though man's inclination is evil from his youth. And I will never again strike down every living thing as I have done" - Genesis 8:20. (Holman Standard Bible)

After that, altars were also erected by Abraham, Isaac, Jacob and then by Moses.[20]

---

[19] www.bible-history.com/sketches/ancient/ancient-altars.html
©Bible History Online

[20] (Refer to Genesis 12:7; 13:4; 22:9; 26:25; 33:20, 35:1,3; Exodus 17:15)

NEW TESTAMENT CORRELATION
- **LOVE**

Just as Abraham built altars, the New Testament believer is supposed to build an altar as well.

Remember, altars were built for *sacrifice* and as a *memorial,* whose fire was never to go out. Therefore, under the New Testament, building an altar is not the erection of a physical structure on which to slaughter and burn animals.

Instead, it is the foundation on which every sacrifice is made; and that foundation is love. When God offered Christ as His Ultimate Sacrifice to shed His royal blood for the sins of humankind, love was His fundamental motivation.

The scripture tells us that,

"God so loved the world that He gave His only begotten son…" - John 3:16a (NASB).

Therefore, **Love** was the reason why God sent His son to the world to redeem humankind. For every service we render to God or to our fellow humans, love has to be at the center and also the driving force.

- **TIME ALONE WITH GOD**

An altar is also synonymous of uninterrupted *"quiet time"* spent alone with God. When Jesus taught His disciples how to pray, He is quoted as saying;
"When you pray, enter into thy closet, and when thou has shut the door, pray to thy father which is in secret; and thy father which sees in secret will reward you openly." Matthew 6:6.

Here, Jesus was establishing the protocol for engaging our Heavenly Father in prayer; which is to spend uninterrupted private time with God.

FORGIVENESS

Another foundation upon which to engage God is walking in forgiveness. While still teaching His disciples the principles on how to pray He says, "If you forgive other people when they sin against you, your Heavenly Father will also forgive you. But if you do not forgive others their sins, your Father will not forgive your sins." -Matthew 6:14-15 (NIV)

Clearly, Jesus was teaching that forgiveness was the foundation or altar on which any form of sacrifice, which includes prayer, had to be laid.

If God will not forgive our sins because we will not forgive others, we have no reason to pray.

The scripture teaches that; if we harbor sin—unforgiveness, bitterness, disobedience—in our hearts, God will not hear us when we call upon Him.

LAID THE WOOD IN ORDER

After building the altar, Abraham laid the wood in order. In Chapter 3, I made a brief reference to the wood which Abraham brought for the burnt offering.

Then in Chapter 5, I shared on the symbolism of the wood, and stated that it represented a myriad of things.

Fundamentally, it was symbolic of *divinely-instituted ordinances* that create the atmosphere for believers to engage the manifest presence of God.

Order in worship is an absolute prerequisite for the manifest presence of God. The scriptures back this fact by stating,
"For God is not a God of disorder but of peace—as in all congregations of the Lord's people."
- 1 Corinthians 14:33 (NIV)

I must admit my pet peeve is disorder and mediocrity in a worship service. Not only do you ruin the service for visitors and members alike, you risk creating a stereotype that can impede the growth of your church or business.

Abraham laying the wood in order before laying his sacrifice on the altar buttresses this argument.

PERICHORESIS

Used to describe the triune relationship between each "person" of the Godhead, "the word itself comes from the Greek *"peri,"* meaning *"around"* and *"chorein,"* meaning *"to give way"* or *"to make room."* Perichoresis could be translated as *"rotation"* or *"going around,"* Some scholars picture this as a sort of choreographed dance." [21]

Speaking of order, there is perfect order with the Triune God. This is reflected in the book of Genesis, where the patriarch Moses gives us a historical account of the order in which Elohim created the universe without any "collision" or "clash."

The Greeks were absolutely right, when they coined the term "perichoresis," giving us an insight into the choreographed dance that goes on between the Father, Son and Holy Spirit.

---

[21] © Copyright © 2011 – 2017. Got Questions Ministries
www.compellingtruth.org – Christian Truth

Understanding this concept is absolutely necessary to appreciate the synergy that emanates from the triune God; which results in perfect order as a result of Perichoresis.

Anything out of order can be said to be in disorder; an irregularity, breach of order, disarray or even clutter.

In medical terms, a disturbance of function, structure or both, resulting from a genetic or embryonic failure in development or from exogenous factors such as poison, trauma, or disease is known as a disorder.[22]

Therefore, science has shown that a disorder can cause an abnormality, known also as a disease.

SLOPPINESS

Sometimes, disorder in the service is a result of lateness, the lack of planning or preparation, or a combination; which results in a sloppy service.

Even when you have skilled musicians arriving late for service, it results in disruption and chaos. If parishioners know not to arrive late at their secular job,

---

[22] http://medicine.academic.ru/118744/primary_mental_disorder

they should know better to be on time and in keeping order for the worship encounter.

There is nothing more fulfilling than attending a service where there was order from the parking lot through to the preacher! Abraham laid the wood in order, before proceeding to lay his sacrifice on the altar.

The panoramic view into heaven, painted by the account of John the revelator, is a clear depiction of order in heaven.

There are the 24 elders who are positioned around God's throne, the crystal glassy sea, and the Lamb of God who was slain from the foundations of the earth.

Then there are Cherubim and Seraphims, whose specific functions are clearly defined to the minutest detail. Clearly, there is the highest precision of orderliness in heaven.

BOUND ISAAC HIS SON

This may sound funny but can you imagine Isaac overpowering his father and taking off, literally running away from his father once he knew that he was the sacrifice?

I know very few people who stare death in the face, without running or trying to escape. I read a sad

Ultimate Sacrifice — Joe Kwapong

but funny story of a man who was so tired of living; he decided to end his life.

He chose to hang himself and as he prepared to do so, he placed a chair directly at the spot where he would climb to commit the heinous suicide. His hope was once the rope was wrapped around his neck; he would voluntarily kick the chair and end his life by strangulation.

When the disgruntled man put the rope around his neck and began to tighten the noose, he felt such discomfort and pain; he began to scream at the top of his lungs as though someone had held a gun to his head to put himself in that predicament.

Fortunately, some of his neighbors overheard the frantic cry for help and as expected, barged in by kicking down the door, and coming to the rescue of this helpless man.

Later, when asked why he had a change of mind, he said "I had no idea how painful strangulation was." I couldn't help but laugh hysterically at this joker.

I am sure that the next time that idea crosses his mind, he would give it a second and probably a third thought, before unwisely trying to end his life.

SUBMISSION

Imagine Isaac being tied, and discovering his life was about to end. He probably would bolt and run. Therefore, the tying of Isaac is synonymous of our willing submission to the purpose of God, which oftentimes goes through a process for His plan to come to pass in our lives.

There are several of God's people who come into the worship experience with their sacrifice untied. There is no voluntary submission to the plan or purpose of God for their lives.

Like the untied animal, they live their personal dream without consulting with God regarding what He would rather have them do.

They are rebellious and unruly; would not submit to authority or take instructions from anyone; literally, they bounce off the wall.

There is therefore the need for our lives to be tied to the Master's will, the hallmark of a true disciple of Christ.

YIELDED LIFE

When Isaac lay on the wood on the altar, it was a clear depiction of Christ; who yielded His life as atonement for sin on Calvary.

The Apostle Paul reminds the New Testament Christian of being a partaker of the suffering of Christ. He states,

"I am crucified with Christ: nevertheless, I live; yet not I, but Christ lives in me: and the life which I now live in the flesh I live by the faith of the Son of God, who loved me, and gave himself for me."
- Galatians 2:20

The ultimate sacrifice is not merely the recitation of liturgical prayer or theatrical exhibition; instead, it is living a "yielded-life" exemplified by the Lord and Savior Jesus Christ.

It is making the courageous choice to live selflessly, and to be reminded that there is only one race—the human race—with whom we must share our talent, treasure and time.

REMEMBER

As New Testament Christians, we have to build lasting altars for sacrifice. An altar of sacrifice is not only limited to prayer; instead, it includes your devotional life.

David writes,

"Oh God, thou art my God; early will I seek thee: my soul thirsts for thee, my flesh longs for thee in a dry and thirsty land, where no water is." - Psalm 63:1

Having a devotional life where the fire on the altar never dies out is part of our reasonable service to God.

Chapter 8
THE ULTIMATE SACRIFICE

"And Abraham stretched forth his hand, and took the knife to slay his son. And the angel of the Lord called unto him out of heaven, and said, Abraham, Abraham: and he said; here am I. And he said, lay not your hand upon the lad, neither do thou anything unto him: now I know that thou fear God, seeing thou hast not withheld thy son, your only son from me."
- (Gen. 22:10-12)

The time had finally come for Abraham to offer the *Ultimate Sacrifice*; and yes his ultimate sacrifice was his son Isaac.

All his preparation for the arduous journey and the actual sacrifice had now reached a crescendo. Was Abraham going to muster the courage to execute God's command?

Or was he going to chicken out, and give a hundred reasons why he could not stand to commit such a violent act of *barbarism*?

Many times we make plans, for instance, on how generous we intend to be if we ever came into sudden wealth and riches like winning the lottery. And by the way, in America, the odds are 1 in 14 million; just in case anyone is considering building a future based on their chances of hitting the jackpot.

So the truth is; although the idea to be generous is a plausible one, the chances of winning and actually carrying out the plan is dismal.

The old adage; "the proof is in the pudding," sums it all up. Therefore, for Abraham to stretch forth his hand in readiness to slay his son, he had to have had unflinching courage, unwavering commitment and resolute trust to carry out God's command.

An outstretched hand or arm signifies the rule of power. This is because the hand or arm has power when it is stretched out.[23]

When Moses expressed doubts about his credentials before Pharaoh—with regard to allowing the children of Israel to leave Egypt, as God had directed him to—this is what God did to affirm Moses.

First, He instructed Moses to cast his rod on the ground, and then it turned into a serpent. Obviously

---

[23] www.biblemeanings.info/words/God/Stretch.htm
E. Swedenborg 1688-1772 I.J Thompson Feb. 2002

astounded, he took to his heels. God asked him to pick it up by the tail; then it became a rod again.

Secondly, God asked Moses to put his hand into his cloak, and when he pulled it out, it had miraculously become smitten with leprosy. Then Moses was asked to repeat the process, after which he was completely healed.

Several times when the children of Israel needed a miracle, God instructed Moses to stretch out his hand or his rod, as a show of God's power and approval on Moses' life.

SACRIFICE IS GIVING

The stretching forth of Abraham's hand is symbolic of unreserved willingness in giving. This gesture typifies a parishioner who is fully committed to giving without reservation, hesitation or complacency.

Offering the *ultimate sacrifice* requires the New Testament believer to be committed to giving. The Scripture says
"There is the one who [generously] scatters [abroad], and yet increases all the more; and there is the one who withholds what is justly due, but it results only in want and poverty." - Proverbs 11:24 (Amplified).

Therefore, we learn from Abraham that the true worship experience involves the stretching forth of our hands. We have to be ready at all times to stretch forth our hands in giving sacrificially.

Whether it is to the poor, taking care of orphans, widows, the less privileged, or to the work of the Lord. Again, the scripture says,
"But to do good and to communicate forget not; for with such sacrifices God is well pleased." – Hebrews 13:16.

THE KNIFE

In Chapter 5, I discussed extensively, the knife and its relevance in the New Testament era. Symbolic of the painful experiences we go through that result in dying to self, not as a result of wrongdoing but as true Disciples of Christ, the knife is an integral part of our Christian walk.

No Christian can escape the knife of affliction for Christ. Considering many brave men and women that have laid down their lives in defense of the gospel, what we consider as challenges in postmodern Christianity pales in comparison.

The slaying of the sacrifice was as equally important as giving the sacrifice. Any sacrifice that had to be placed on the altar had to be killed before being offered as a burnt offering to God.

Can you imagine a ram, sheep, or a lamp on the altar of sacrifice; fully alive? Not only would this be cruel to burn the animal alive, it would be impossible to keep the animal on the altar, as it will attempt frantically to escape the fire.

As you can see, there was a good reason why the animal being sacrificed, first had to be slain. Yet as New Testament believers, we violate the same principle when we are not fully yielded to God, in worship.

When you suffer for the gospel's sake, it is as offering the *ultimate sacrifice* to God. With that kind of sacrifice, God is well pleased.

The Scripture says
"So put to death and deprive of power the evil longings of your earthly body [with its sensual, self-centered instincts] immorality, impurity, sinful passion, evil desire, and greed, which is [a kind of] idolatry [because it replaces your devotion to God." - Col. 3:5. (Amplified)

The knife is also synonymous of the experiences we go through in life, designed to humble and render us broken before God. Remember the Scripture says,

"The sacrifices of God are a broken spirit: a broken and a contrite heart, O God, thou wilt not despise." - Psalm 51:17.

1st ANGELIC CALL

In Chapter 10, I discuss angelic visitation in worship, where there is a greater exposition on the subject. Under this sub-heading, my emphasis is the angel who delivered this message of goodwill to Abraham.

I would therefore encourage you to read Chapter 10 for in-depth information on angels in general.

Bible scholars and theologians are divided when it comes to the identity of the angel Abraham encountered at Moriah.

This is partly because there is not enough information to explicitly identify that angel. There are those who espouse both visitations to have been carried out by a created angel or messenger from God.

They assert this position based on the fact that the Hebrew word used for "the angel of the Lord" is "malak YHWH" both times.

However, I subscribe to those who argue otherwise. The reason being fifty-six times, the phrase "the angel of the Lord" appears in fifty-one verses in the Hebrew Bible. [24]

Whenever that phrase was used to describe the sighting of "the angel of the Lord," He spoke, identified and exercised the responsibilities of God.

Those individuals, who saw the angel of the Lord, were afraid for their lives because they had *"seen the Lord."*

The Scripture says,
"But He said, you cannot see my face, for no one may see me and live." - Exodus 33:20 (NIV)

In Genesis 16:7-12, we read about the first story of the angel of the Lord appearing to Hagar, as she fled the wrath of Sarah, into the wilderness.

The "angel" disclosed to Hagar that she was pregnant with a son, admonished her to return home, and said her son would be called Ishmael.[25]

4 REASONS

There are 4 reasons why you should absolutely be convinced that "the angel of the Lord" was a pre-

---

[24] www.christinprophecy.org/articles/the-angel-of-the-lord/
[25] www.christinprophecy.org/articles/the-angel-of-the-lord/
©2017 Lamb & Lion Ministries.

incarnate Christ and not referring to any other created angelic being.

1. "No man has seen God at any time; the only begotten son, who is in the bosom of the father, he hath declared him." - John 1:18

2. When "the angel of the Lord" appeared to Moses in the burning bush, He told Moses,
"I am the God of thy father, the God of Abraham, the God of Isaac, and the God of Jacob. Moses hid his face; for he was afraid to look upon God." –
Exodus 3:6
No created angel speaks, identifies and exercises the responsibilities of God the way this angel does.

3. The apostle Paul argues that God dwells in light, which no man can approach, whom no man has seen, nor can see. (1 Timothy 6:16)

4. With the exception of the King James Version of Matthew 28:2; which other translations do not translate as such, "The angel of the Lord" is no longer mentioned, and ceases to appear in the New Testament after the incarnation of Jesus Christ. [26]

---

[26] www.google.com/amps/s/
www.gotquestions.org/amp/angel-of-the-Lord.htmi ©Copyright 2002-2016 Got Questions Ministries

Therefore, the angel of the Lord was a pre-incarnate appearance of Christ; known also as Christophany. Remember the scripture states,
"And God said you cannot see my face; for there shall no man see me and live." - Exodus 33:20

As New Testament believers, we should never go into the holy place without sensitivity to the Holy Spirit.

Like Christ, the Holy Spirit still speaks to us today. The worship experience should never be mundane, or performed out of a sense of obligation.

Instead, it has to be engaged out of a sense of having a relationship with God.

DISCERNING HIS VOICE IN WORSHIP

When Abraham set out for Moriah three days earlier, he had his marching orders. A close look at his work ethic reveals a man who takes pride in fostering and maintaining hard work.

However, the one thing Abraham had was flexibility and sensitivity in discerning the voice of God. Had he been rigid and insensitive to God's leading, he probably would have sacrificed his son, when God had changed the plan.

Worship leaders, especially, necessarily need to have the spirit of discernment. If you lead people in corporate worship, and you are unable to discern the leading of the Holy Spirit, I suggest you take the time to pray for the Lord to grant you the spirit of discernment.

Part of the problem is that we live in such a world where people want to be in and out. Preachers have to go through their presentation in record time.

Everything is so fast-paced, failure to stick to rigid timelines or staying abreast with the times mean you risk losing your "clientele."

When was the last time we took the time to engage God in worship? Do we just follow a routine, or are we sensitive to discern His leading?

As worship leaders or psalmists who lead God's people into His presence, it is incumbent upon us to cultivate the skill of sensitivity to the leading of the Holy Spirit.

Again, I challenge every worshiper and worship leader to take the time to prepare thoroughly, like Abraham did. I also want to entreat the minstrels—those who play musical instruments—as well as the sound engineers, to spend time perfecting their craft.

There is nothing as distractive and repulsive as musicians who either arrive late for corporate worship, or have poor skills. It is simply a reflection of the value people place on the service.

Finally, let's learn to cultivate the habit of observing silence during our time of worship, to listen for the voice of God.

NOW I KNOW

"Now I know" sounds like a ridiculous assertion for the angel of the Lord to make, considering He possessed the all-knowing qualities as the Father.

After all, when He was first introduced in the Old Testament, He foretold Hagar of the conception and birth of her son, and gave his name as Ishmael.

Also, when He appeared to Manoah and his wife, He ascended in the flame as Manoah offered burn offerings that blazed toward heaven.

Unlike the angel of the Lord, all created angels are barred from receiving worship. Therefore, He was the pre-incarnation of Christ, who possessed foreknowledge.

As a result, the statement; "for now I know," is an oxymoron. A concealed principle, crafted to reveal an enduring truth regarding true worship.

When the angel of the Lord made this statement, it was as if to say; you have proved beyond the shadow of a doubt; you have passed the test! In other words, Abraham's actions had validated what God knew about him all this while.

Think for instance about a sacred principle in the American criminal justice system asserting that a defendant is innocent until proven guilty.

The burden of proof therefore, lies squarely on the shoulders of the prosecution. To draw a parallel, the angel of the Lord is not the prosecution who needs to prove Abraham's guilt, or the jury who is waiting for evidence to convict or acquit.

Rather, the burden of proof was upon Abraham, to prove his unflinching faith in God. Remember, this entire episode started out with God testing Abraham's loyalty, in order to promote and not to embarrass him.

WHAT THIS MEANS

The lesson here is that we will be tested on all fronts, but have the responsibility of proving ourselves. It is not good enough to say; "God knows my heart, and He understands my situation." We would have to demonstrate our love and commitment to God, just like Abraham; who did not simply parrot his affection and trust in God, but actually demonstrated what was in his heart.

To refuse to be tested is to refuse to be promoted. We have already established that God tests us to prove our loyalty in order to endorse and promote us.

In other words, it is for our benefit that we are tested, so that when we have been tried, as the Bible says, we would come out like fine gold.

The problem is everybody wants the gold but very few want to pay the price. Just like in the Olympics, those who win gold put in the extra work, while some others look for the easiest way out.

I pray that in our quest to seek God on the holy hills of worship, we would be willing, like Abraham, to stretch forth our hands to offer the *ultimate sacrifice.* We should be sensitive to the directions of the Holy Spirit, and demonstrate loyalty to God beyond reasonable doubt, so He would be pleased with us.

Chapter 9
DIVINE PROVISION IN WORSHIP

*"And Abraham lifted up his eyes, and looked, and behold behind him a ram caught in a thicket by his horns: and Abraham went and took the ram, and offered him up for a burnt offering in the stead of his son. And Abraham called the name of that place Jehovah Jireh: as it is said to this day, in the mount of the Lord it shall be seen". - (*Genesis 22:13-14).

Just as Abraham lifted his eyes, New Testament believers need to cultivate the habit of worshiping with our eyes wide opened.

By that, I am not implying the opening of our physical eyes during the time of worship. I am referring to having the consciousness of God's divine presence in the time of worship.

This is the kind of consciousness that maintains a heightened sense of expectation; as though you were driving behind a school bus, and expecting the driver to make frequent stops to pick children up.

The lifting up of our head or eyes is indicative of not being oblivious or insensitive to the possibility of receiving revelation during the time of worship.

Therefore, to worship with your eyes wide open is to worship with the awareness that God gives instructions during the time of worship; sometimes in contrast to long-held pre-conceptions and prejudices.

Secondly, the lifting of the eyes is indicative of dependency on God.

The Scripture declares,
"I will lift up my eyes unto the hills from where comes my help? My help comes from the Lord which made heaven and earth." -Psalms 121:1-2.

Whenever we engage God in worship, we need to come into His presence with an attitude of total dependency on Him, as worship is coming to the place of complete surrender and total reliance on this awesome God.

A place you know you are helpless without this magnificent God. We don't have to put on that attitude only when we are in need—a paradigm I call *"the spare-tire mentality."*

The spare-tire mentality is treating God just like we treat our spare-tire; you never stop to think about it until you have a flat tire or have need of it.

When you expect a guest from out of town for instance, and several hours go by without you hearing from them, you tend to be nervous; possibly becoming agitated.

It accentuates especially when you keep calling them, but they wouldn't answer or return your call. A barrage of thoughts goes through your mind, and unless you keep a positive attitude, you can imagine the unthinkable.

In the same vein, when your expectations seem to go unmet for a long time, there is a tendency to begin to have doubts about whether God hears your prayers at all.

In spite of what may look like a delay or uncertainty, you would have to still learn to keep your eyes lifted up.

I don't claim ownership over this recommendation, but that is part of what we glean from Abraham, in lifting up his eyes to look for provision in the time of worship.

LOOK BEHIND YOU

I find it very ironic that Abraham had come to a pivotal point in his life where all he had to do to resolve the myriad of challenges he was dealing with at the time, was simply to look behind him.

Remember he was facing the trial of his faith; which had to be handled with such dexterity, failure of which could result in complications such as being charged with murder, jail time, divorce, a psychiatric evaluation with a possible misdiagnosis of schizophrenia, and being ostracized from his community.

Yet the scripture says he *"lifted up his eyes, and looked behind him"* and there was the solution! Has it occurred to you why the medical profession takes time to collect data on medical history?

This is because there is a direct correlation between our past and our future. Sometimes, the solution to a current problem is a direct result of a choice we made in the past.

If we would take the time to examine the past, we can rectify the present, and brace ourselves for a better future.

Let's not forget; had Abraham been rigid, insensitive and insistent on carrying out God's initial order to sacrifice his son, without an openness and flexibility to examine himself and his past i.e. —

looking behind him—he could have lost sight of the substitute God had prepared for him.

In spite of his fervor to please God, Abraham would have sacrificed his son without realizing he had completely missed out on change; change that comes as a result of self-examination and sober reflection.

ABILITY TO CHANGE

Deepak Chopra is quoted as saying, *"all great changes are preceded by chaos."*

I couldn't agree more. Change can be very unsettling; especially when one is committed to a cause.

While dutifully carrying out his orders, God interrupted Abraham and gave him a different set of instructions.

Thankfully, Abraham held his peace, and upon careful examination of his surroundings, discovered God had provided a ram in the bush, nearby.

The provision could not have come at a better time; as God is always on time. The scripture says, "He has made everything beautiful in its time."– Ecclesiastes 3:11a (ESV).

My fascination with this part of the story is with Abraham's ability to switch, or change while in mainstream.

Remember, had he been insistent on maintaining the initial instructions he had received three days prior and refused to change, he would have been starring at a dead son, unduly sacrificed. I therefore believe that a true worshiper has to be sensitive enough to perceive, flexible enough to change, and humble enough to learn new things.

DIVINE PROVISION

Not only did Abraham lift up his eyes, he looked and saw a ram *"caught in a thicket by its horns."* After seeing God's supernatural provision of the ram, he proceeded to take and substitute it as a burnt offering to Him. Just as the ram was the substitute for Isaac, God gave the world a substitute in the person of Christ.

Now, this single divine act was the textbook definition of divine provision. If in doubt whether the angel of the Lord actually appeared to Abraham, try grappling with the unlikely event of a ram being caught at the same time and place where Abraham was so close to sacrificing his son.

I have and continue to experience divine provision myself, and could write volumes on the subject.

Dating back nearly four decades, I lost my dad as a kid. My mother was left to raise six children without a job.

Yet, through God's provision, we did not only survive in a country whose economy was in tatters at the time, we thrived by educating ourselves through college without any government handout.

Many times, God has miraculously provided for my family, when we have depleted all our resources; and I do mean all of our resources.

My older daughter is a Gates Millennium scholar. This means she gets to be educated to the postgraduate level, without paying a dime for college!

Let it be said, though, that she will repay her debt to society, and to this great nation, in order to ensure that others would also have the same opportunity afforded her.

Not only that, every waking morning is God's divine provision of brand-new mercies, laced with an invaluable opportunity to right every wrong.

Clearly, God had rewarded Abraham's faith in Him and made divine provision for him as well.

Instead of killing Isaac, God replaced him with an animal.

The substitution of Isaac with a ram is indicative of Jesus Christ being made a substitute for the sins of the world.

The Scripture says;
"God so loved the world, that he gave his only son, that whosoever, believed in his name, should not perish but have eternal life." – John 3:16.

The selfless sacrifice of Jesus Christ was the *Ultimate Sacrifice* which essentially was propitiation offered to God.

The world needed redemption, but the sacrifice had to be of the highest quality to appease God. A modern-day example would be an offender who commits a heinous crime, whose sentencing must be proportional to their crime.

A judge essentially sentences the criminal, based on the merits of the case. When the perpetrator serves their sentence, and fully satisfies the court, they are then released into the community as having served their punishment. Satisfaction of the law is equivalent to propitiation offered to God.

Similarly, Jesus served time and paid the *Ultimate Sacrifice* for the sin of high treason, committed by the first couple God created.

Because humankind is one family, the sin of the first family was imputed on the human race. Just as there is family inheritance, we inherited the sinful nature of the first family.

Remember, in the biblical story of the brothers Cain and Abel, Cain murdered Abel yet there is no record of Cain witnessing a murder prior to him committing the crime.

Sin had invaded God's creation, resulting in the degenerate state of the heart. Therefore, it was only a matter of time, for sin to be made manifest. Jesus took the place of our sins and died in our stead.

Therefore, as we learn to lift up our heads in expectation and total dependency on God, coupled with looking "behind" us in sober reflection in the time of worship, God will always grant us divine provision.

Focus on life's many blessings and not its burdens. See the bountiful provision God has made, and not the problems you face.

Lift up your eyes in great hope of faith and optimism, and not cynicism. Learn to focus on the

Lord rather than your seemingly-insurmountable challenges.

Remember, Abraham exemplified the New Testament believer who must seek solutions rather than focusing on setbacks.

IN THE MOUNTAIN OF THE LORD

The story of God's supernatural provision for Abraham at *"the mountain of the Lord"* in Moriah, became so popularized that a transformational proverb was adapted,

"In the mountain of the Lord it shall be seen." – (Genesis 22:14c.)

"It" here refers to God's divine provision; depending on what your need is at the time.

In other words, God will always ensure provision on "the mountain of the Lord," no matter how great your need is. Remember He is the all-sufficient One.

What a prophetic word to the Body of Christ today!!! We can replicate Abraham's results if we would follow his example, and do exactly as he did.

Science informs us that mountains are the result of tectonic forces or volcanism. Over 565 times, "mountains" and "hills" are mentioned in the Bible.

They were also simply a part of the ancient biblical landscape, spread throughout the land. In spite of this phenomenon, mountains have always had meaningful significance in the Bible.

In modern-day lingo, a *"mountain-top experience"* refers to a life-changing, rejuvenating, personal encounter with God.

Because of their height, mountains have been viewed as being "closer to God."

In the Old Testament, Moses received the Ten Commandments on Mount Sinai and upon his return after forty days and nights, his mountain-top encounter with God was so spectacular his face shone with the glory of God's presence. After the death of Moses, God buried him in Mount Nebo.

The riveting story of Elijah and the 450 prophets of Baal, where the former challenged the false prophets to a showdown, was settled on Mount Carmel.

After gathering twelve stones to represent each of the twelve Tribes of Israel, Elijah rebuilt the altar, which had been torn down.

Now, at the time of the evening sacrifice, Elijah walked up to the altar and prayed. Immediately, fire fell from heaven and consumed the sacrifice.

Baal's false prophets had failed to ignite theirs and this settled the argument that the God of Elijah was indeed the Most-High.

At the transfiguration of Jesus in the New Testament, Moses and Elijah appeared on a mountain where Jesus went to pray with Peter, John and James.

Jesus' temptation, the beatitudes (also known as "the Sermon on the Mount"), the commissioning of the disciples, the feeding of the 5000, and the crucifixion of Jesus, all took place on a mount.

Also, many times, Jesus went up a mountain to find solitude to pray.

LESSON

Based on all the overwhelming evidence, although God is omniscient, spending quality time in seclusion—away from every distraction—is a very effective way of engaging God.

He is absolutely not confined to a mount; Jesus made that abundantly clear when he had a discourse with the woman at the well in John 4.

However, if Jesus spent quality time praying on a mount, I have no qualms doing the same. While I am there, my focus is to have a divine encounter, away from a world of untold distractions, understanding there is divine provision in worship.

PRAYER

Beloved, I pray for you that whatever your needs are—whether they are emotional or physical healing, deliverance, a financial break, power to overcome grief, a sound mind to make sound judgment—the God of Abraham would touch and restore you, right now! May every need be supplied, according to God's riches in Christ Jesus.

I pray the same God, who provided a ram as a substitute for Isaac, provide for every need in your life. May Jehovah Jireh show Himself strong and mighty on your behalf, as He teaches you to trust Him; in Jesus' name, Amen!

Chapter 10
ANGELIC VISITATION IN WORSHIP

"And the angel of the Lord called unto Abraham out of heaven the second time, and said, by myself have I sworn, says the Lord, for because thou hast done this thing, and hast not withheld thy son, your only son." - (Gen. 22:15-16)

I am greatly persuaded that burnt offerings get God's undivided attention. When I wrote about the history of burnt offerings in Chapter 2, I mentioned Genesis 8:20 as the very first recorded account in the Bible, and stated God's reaction as to it well.

After the flood, the scripture informs us that,
"The LORD smelled a sweet savor; and the LORD said in his heart, I will not again curse the ground any more for man's sake; for the imagination of man's heart is evil from his youth; neither will I again smite any more everything living, as I have done." - Genesis 8:21

God responded to Abraham's sacrifice with the same intensity he did Noah's. Yet there are very few incidents recorded in the Scriptures that captivated God's exclusive attention the way burnt offerings did.

I entreat the New Testament church to engage the King of the universe the way Abraham did; and we are bound to have an encounter that will transform the Church, and our world.

Speaking of angelic visitation, there are enough angels to go around. The Bible states;
"Then I looked and heard the voice of many angels, numbering thousands upon thousands, and ten thousand times ten thousand. They encircle the throne, and the living Creatures and the elders."- Revelations 5:11

The sighting of angelic beings on earth during the time of sacrifice, or true worship is not unusual. "Angels are created beings and ministering spirits, who are normally invisible, but can manifest themselves to humans."[27]

Sent forth as special agents from God, their assignment is to carry out specific missions and

---

[27] www.christinprophecy.org/articles/the-ministry-of-angels
© 2017 Lamb & Lion Ministries

extraordinary tasks, while the vast majority worships the Creator of the universe in awe."[28]

The book of Hebrews states that,

"Are not all angels ministering spirits sent to serve those who will inherit salvation?"–Hebrews 1:14 (NIV).

"There are various categories of celestial beings with different characteristics and roles such as Seraphim, Cherubims and Archangels who perform special tasks.

SERAPHIM

"The word "seraphim" (singular is seraph) is probably a translation of 'fiery ones' and probably stems from the fiery imagery often associated with the Presence of God.

"Seraphim stood above Him, each having six wings; with two he covered his face, and with two he covered his feet, and with two he flew." (Isaiah 6:2).

---

[28] www.carm.org/are-there-different-kinds-of-angels-in-the-bibleAchtemeier, Paul J., Th.D., Harper's Bible Dictionary, (San Francisco: Harper and Row, Publishers, Inc.) 1985

CHERUBIM

Cherubim are typically represented with wings, feet, and hands but are also described in different forms as having two faces (Ezek. 41:18) and even four faces (Ezek. 10:21).

Cherubim were considered to be angels that guarded sacred things. In Gen. 3:24 they guarded the tree of life.

They were over the Ark of the Covenant on the Mercy Seat (1 Sam. 4:4). See also Psalm 80:1; 99:1.

Figures of Cherubs were embroidered on the temple veil (Exodus 26:31; 2 Chron. 3:7) and lavished Solomon's temple (1 Kings 6:26ff).

"So he drove out the man; and he placed at the east of the garden of Eden Cherubims, and a flaming sword which turned every way, to keep the way of the tree of life." (Gen. 3:24). See also Exodus 25:18-22; Hebrews 9:5.

ARCHANGEL

The word "archangel" is not found in the Old Testament. References to Michael the archangel appear only in 1 Thess. 4:16 and Jude 1:9.

However, Gabriel, who is considered an archangel, appears in both the Old Testament and New

Testament. In the Old he is found in Dan. 8:15-26 and 9:21-27.

In the New he is mentioned in Luke 1:11-20, 26-38. He seems to be a messenger angel. On the other hand, Michael the archangel seems to be a warrior angel (Rev. 12:7) who does battle (Dan. 10:13, 21; 12:1).

An interesting note is that in Romans 8:38, Ephesians 1:21 and Colossians 1:16, the word 'principalities' is used. In Greek, the word has the prefix of *Arche* suggesting archangel. Some think this means there is a hierarchy of angels as is suggested in 1 Peter 3:22, "who is at the right hand of God, having gone into heaven, after angels and authorities and powers had been subjected to Him."

"For the Lord shall descend from heaven with a shout, with the voice of the archangel, and with the trump of God: and the dead in Christ shall rise first," - (1 Thessalonians 4:16).

RULERS AND POWERS

It is not known if these are a true class of angels or if it is just an expression describing the power of angels.

If they are in reference to an angelic rank of some sort, nothing is known of their purpose and appearance.

The Bible says
"For our struggle is not against flesh and blood, but against the rulers, against the powers, against the world forces of this darkness, against the spiritual forces of wickedness in the heavenly places."– Ephesians 6:12 NASB95

FALLEN ANGELS

Fallen angels are those who, with Satan, rebelled against God before the fall of Adam and Eve. Most Christian scholars agree that one-third of the angels fell. The Bible says,
"And another sign appeared in heaven: and behold, a great red dragon having seven heads and ten horns, and on his heads were seven diadems.   - (Revelations 12:3).

The fallen ones await an ultimate and final judgment, "For if God spared not the angels that sinned, but cast them down to hell, and delivered them into chains of darkness, to be reserved unto judgment;" (2 Peter 2:4)."[29]

There are 5 angels mentioned specifically by name, who are;

GABRIEL

First there is Gabriel; an archangel who introduces himself in Luke 1:19 as "Gabriel, who stands in the presence of God," whose job appears to be one that carries messages from God.

We are first introduced to him when he appeared to Daniel as a man, who revealed the meaning of a vision to Daniel.

Secondly, while serving during his turn as High Priest on the Day of Atonement in the Temple, the archangel Gabriel appeared to Zachariah, and announced the birth of his son John the Baptist.

About six months later, he appeared to Mary the mother of Jesus, proclaiming she would be the mother of the Savior.

---

[29] www.carm.org/are-there-different-kinds-of-angels-in-the-bible Slick, Matt. "Are there different kinds of angels in the bible?" Christian Apologetics and Research Ministry Achtemeier, Paul J., Th.D., Harper's Bible Dictionary, (San Francisco: Harper and Row, Publishers, Inc.) 1985

MICHAEL

Then there is Michael; also an archangel whose name means; "Who is like God?"

Archangel Michael appears to be the one who wages war against Satan and his angels.

A fighting machine does not come close to describing the prowess of this archangel.

The book of Revelations reports,
"There was a war in heaven, Michael and his angels waging war with the dragon. The dragon and his angels waged war…and there was no longer a place found for them in heaven." Revelation 12:7-8.

When the prince of the kingdom of Persia—a demonic celestial being—appeared to withstand Gabriel from delivering a message from God, Michael came to his rescue and prevailed.

This same archangel also stands guard over the nation Israel, and has a prophetic task of delivering the children of Israel during

"…a time of distress such as never occurred since there was a nation until that time…"
- Daniel 12:1.

SATAN/DRAGON

Once known as Lucifer, before pride was found in his heart, Satan is the fallen archangel who rebelled against God. Cast away from heaven by the Archangel Michael; "There was no place found in heaven for him and his cohorts."

During the temptation of Jesus Christ in the wilderness for forty days and nights, Satan tempted Him "at every point" yet Christ did not yield to sin or the devil. While Jesus was "with the wild beasts, the angels ministered to Him." Mark 1:13

As the master of disguise, Satan "disguises himself as the angel of light." However, the apostle Paul says; "The God of peace will soon crush Satan under your feet."

As the father of all lies and liars, he is also the master of deception, and the "great dragon" who will be "thrown down, the serpent of old who is called the devil and Satan, who deceives the whole world..." Revelation 12:9

BEELZEBUB

Beelzebub is interpreted as "Lord of the flies," sometimes attributed to Satan in the New Testament as one of his names.

King Ahaziah fell through his lattice in his upper chamber and became ill. He then sent messengers to go inquire of Beelzebub, the god of Ekron, whether he would die from his injuries, or he would recover.

In the long run, Elijah brought the king a word from the Lord that, because he had not inquired of the Lord, but had done so from Beelzebub, he was going to die. The king did according to the word of the Lord through the prophet.

In Mark 3:22; the scribes who came down from Jerusalem were accusing Christ of being possessed by Beelzebub and casting demons by the ruler of the demons.

Visibly offended, Jesus asked the age-old question; "can a house divided against itself stand?"

ABADDON/APOLLYON

Last but not least, the Book of Revelations speaks of Abaddon as the angel of the bottomless pit who appears to be a ruler of evil spirits. [30]

---

[30] www.carm.org/names-of-angels-in-bible
Slick, Matt. President and Founder. What are the names of the angels in the Bible? The Christian Apologetics and Research Ministry

"They have as king over them, the angel of the abyss; His name in Hebrew is Abaddon, and in the Greek he has the name Apollyon." --Revelation 9:11

SECOND CHANCE

When the angel, announcing God's intent to overwhelmingly bless Abraham and his seed called out a second time, it was clear that Abraham's unquestioned obedience and unwavering commitment to offer his son Isaac had met God's approval.

I can tell you categorically that, God will always respond to the *ultimate sacrifice* that meets the standards exemplified by Abraham.

It is worthy of note that the angel of the Lord called a second time.

There is always a second chance for every missed opportunity with God—double for every trouble—if we will engage God rightly.

If we will step out in total obedience just as the Abraham did, I guarantee we will encounter the God of Abraham the same way he did.

IMMUTABILITY OF GOD

When something is said to be immutable, it is unchanging over time or unable to be changed. God does not need disclosure to change His position on a subject matter.

Neither does He need to improve upon Himself, as he is perfect in all His ways. Therefore, the immutability of God is His quality of not changing; unlike humankind who do.

The Bible declares,
"For I am the Lord, I change not..." - Malachi 3:6a.

Due to the fact that God is eternal and exists outside the constraints of time, He is fixed, permanent, and unchangeable.

As a result of this nature, God did not have to swear to Abraham; He absolutely had nothing to prove. However, God was so moved by Abraham's selfless sacrificial giving. In human terms, He was simply blown away.

In this day and age, the practice of offering animals as a burnt offering to God has changed, but the principles that define the quality of our seed remain unchanged.

If New Testament believers will bear in mind the immutability of God is related to His omniscience—being all knowing—we will engage God with a renewed attitude to which God will respond akin to Abraham's.

10 FACTS ABOUT ANGELS

1. Angels—good and bad—and everything else in the "heavenly realm," whether thrones or powers were created by Christ. (ref: Colossians 1:16-18)

2. "With the exception of special angels, most references to angels in the Bible say nothing about wings, and in passages like Genesis 18-19, it is certain that no wings were visible."[31]

3. Only unique angels like Seraphims have 6 wings. (ref. Isaiah 6:2)

4. "Angels are mentioned at least 108 times in the Old Testament and 165 times in the New Testament."[32]

5. Angels rejoiced when God laid the foundations of the earth. (ref. Job 38:7)

6. Children have been assigned angels. (ref. Matthew 18:10)

7. Angels are spirits, sent as agents to serve and protect those who shall be heirs of salvation. (ref. Hebrews 1:14)

---

[31] www.christiananswers.net/q-acb/acb-t005.html
Dr. John Bechtle "Do angels have wings? Ref Genesis 18-19
[32] Dr. Paul Eymann. "Who or what are angels?" Chafer, Systematic Theology, II, 3.

8. Unbeknown to some, they have entertained angels. Possibly because angels have been known to take on human form. (ref. Hebrews 13:2)

9. Angels are NOT to be worshipped. However, Satan sought to be worshiped. This was part of the reason why he was deposed from heaven. *(Refer to Revelations 19:10; Ezekiel 28:17 & 18)*

10. Whenever a believer begins to entreat God through petition or worship, there is audience with God. However, angels face resistance sometimes through the power of the air while delivering answers. (-Ephesians. 6:2,12, Daniel 10:13).

Remember, angels are activated when Christians truly seek to engage God the way Abraham did, in offering the *ultimate sacrifice* to God.

Chapter 11
GOD RECIPROCATES IN WORSHIP

"That in blessing I will bless thee, and in multiplying I will multiply thy seed as the stars of the heaven, and as the sand which is upon the sea shore; and thy seed shall possess the gate of his enemies; And in thy seed shall all the nations of the earth be blessed; because thou hast obeyed my voice." -Genesis 22:17-18

It was about 9 o'clock in the evening when I pulled up in the driveway.

Usually, all the lights inside the house would be switched off, except the florescent outside which we keep on through the night.

However, on this fateful evening, I could see the lights turned on through the blinds—which would have been drawn.

As I got out of my car and headed for the front door of the house, I knew my subwoofer was at the verge of giving up the ghost.

With every step I took towards the door, the sound of throbbing music got louder and louder. Finally, after picking out the right key, I stuck it in the keyhole, turned the knob and thrust the door wide open.

Like mice nibbling on cheese in the dark or nocturnal animals enjoying scraps of food, my daughters and their unscrupulous guests were having a field day at my house, unauthorized and unsupervised.

For the first thirty seconds, I stood at the entrance spellbound, in utter disbelief. What would possess these *"ninkapums"* to believe they could pull such a stunt?

Shortly afterwards, I regained my composure and yelled at the top of my lungs, sending the party fleeing helter-skelter across the room as mice scampering at the intrusion of bright light.

After the dust settled, my daughters were grounded for a week. I sent them to work the next day; scrubbing the entire house and restoring it to its *former glory*.

"Why should we have to do all this work alone?" my younger daughter asked. "Let our friends come and help us clean up." she demanded.

That left me no choice but to pull my philosophy extraordinaire hat to which I said, Criss Jami, the American poet, essayist, and existentialist philosopher born Christopher James Gilbert, is quoted as saying;

"If you build the guts to do something, anything, then you better save enough to face the consequences."

CHOICES HAVE CONSEQUENCES

Looking back at the story of my daughters and their unauthorized party, I can see a direct correlation between the effect of their actions and Abraham's.

Although Abraham's actions were upright, Robert G. Ingersoll's observation that "in nature, there are neither rewards nor punishments; there are consequences;" could not be more true, as both actions had dire consequences.

In the case with my daughters, they bore the brunt of my ire as their punishment for organizing the party. While their friends were home *chilling*, they were left to deal with the heat and gravity of the situation.

I WILL BLESS YOU

An act of self-denial and submissive obedience by Abraham had resulted in divine favor, and the reaffirmation of the covenant God made with him.

We are told Terah, Abraham's father, migrated with Abram and certain members of his kinfolk from Ur of the Chaldeans and settled in Haran—where Terah later died. This is significant because certain theologians argue that this was the period Abram received his first call.

By the second time God appeared to Abram in Genesis 12:1-3, his name was still unchanged. Terah had passed, and God instructed him to move out of Haran—the city in which he, his father and clan had sought refuge—to a new location He would later show Abram.

God then establishes the covenant with Abram, and gives him more details regarding the covenant. By the time Abram made the pilgrimage to Moriah, God had changed his name to Abraham, and revealed more details about the covenant.

This sequence of events establishes the fact that revelation is progressive; never exposed in one instance.

Pleased with Abraham's *Ultimate Sacrifice*, God promises to bless him, and confirms it with an oath; a solemn reminder that those willing to sacrifice anything for God will receive a fitting reward.

As God cannot lie, it was unnecessary for Him to have taken an oath to stand by His word. The simple fact that He declared His intentions to bless Abraham was good enough to establish credibility.

However, to assure the New Testament believer that God reciprocates in worship, and will not renege on His promise, He took an oath. This is what true worship will do.

MULTIPLY YOUR SEED

In addition to the assurance of a personal blessing, God guaranteed Abraham a generational blessing. This was clearly the result of Abraham's unquestioning obedience to unreservedly offer his *Ultimate Sacrifice* to God.

Even though God appreciates our sacrifices, He honors our obedience the more. How could God deny Abraham any kind of blessing after this selfless act of obedience?

God reminded Abraham of His promise to him saying, "Indeed I will greatly bless you, and I will greatly multiply your seed as the stars of the heaven, and as the sand which is on the seashore, and your seed shall possess the gate of their enemies"- Genesis 22:17 (NASB)

NATURAL SEED

The multiplication of Abraham's seed was both to his natural and spiritual descendants. His natural descendants included both Jews and Arabs. Through his older son Ishmael, whose mother was Hagar the handmaid of Sarah, Ishmaelites were born.

He was an archer who became a prominent figure in Islam; the ancestor of the Prophet Mohammad. Although Abraham sent Hagar and her son away, they left with an inheritance of God's generational blessing.

God pledged to make Ishmael a great nation of people, with wealth and riches in their land. He was also blessed with twelve sons, who became the descendants of many nations.

This act of God proves that although Ishmael was not the son He promised to bless Abraham and Sarah with, God blessed him anyway. This was because Ishmael was the seed of Abraham.

Isaac was the natural promised seed of Abraham and Sarah. Younger than his half-brother Ishmael, he was the only child of Abraham and Sarah.

At age one hundred, Abraham and Sarah only had one child—Isaac. Yet, God had promised to multiply their seed. How long was it going to take to fulfill God's promise to multiply their seed?

Were Abraham and Sarah going to live long enough to inherit the promise?

In spite of this seeming impossibility, God was true to His word.

Isaac and his wife Rebecca gave birth to Esau and Jacob. Later, God changed Jacob's name to Israel, and blessed him with twelve sons who became the twelve tribes of Israel.

God's promise of multiplying Abraham's seed was gradually coming into fruition. Remember God had taken an oath, and sworn by Himself to fulfill His promise to Abraham.

Literally, God was bound by His word and could simply not renege. Abraham's blessings were guaranteed to happen.

SPIRITUAL SEED

Those who come to God, through the Messiah, can also become the spiritual seed of Abraham and enjoy the full benefit of the Abrahamic covenant. To give credence to this concept, the scripture says,

"Now, God made his promises to Abraham and to his descendant. The scripture does not use the plural "descendants," meaning many people, but the singular "descendant," meaning one person only, namely, Christ." - Galatians 3:16 (GNT)

This means whether you are African, Asian, or American; rich, poor, Democrat, Progressive or Republican, Arab, Jew, or Muslim, as long as you receive Jesus Christ as your Lord and Savior, you become the seed of Christ, who qualifies you as a seed of Abraham. The scripture says,

"If you belong to Christ, then you are Abraham's seed, and heirs according to the promise." - Galatians 3:29

Therefore, Abraham's spiritual descendants are partakers of the inheritance of the blessings God pronounced on his seed.

This is the basis for Gentiles—people, who are not natural descendants of Abraham—to be drafted as heirs of the promise.

As stated earlier, to become a spiritual descendant, one must receive God's *Ultimate Sacrifice* for the sin of humankind.

The Bible states,

"Understand, then, that those who believe are children of Abraham." - Galatians 3:7

This was exactly how the promise God made to Abraham was going to be fulfilled. The Gentiles were going to receive the promise through the seed of Eve, whom God said would bruise the head of the serpent.

STARS AND SAND

It is fascinating the manner in which Moses—the writer of the book of Genesis—metaphorically describes the innumerable seed God promised to the patriarch Abraham. The scripture says,

"...I will multiply thy seed as the stars of the heaven, and as the sand which is upon the seashore,"
- Genesis 22:17a

According to the NASA website, our galaxy—the Milky Way—has roughly one hundred billion stars. Yet, the Milky Way is not the only galaxy in the universe.

Arguably, the number of grains of sand on all the beaches on planet earth is equal to this number—one hundred billion.

Not only is this shocking, it gives us a unique insight into the incredulous awe of Yahweh, the Creator of the universe.

It is also reported that there are approximately ten billion galaxies found in the observable universe.

The number of stars in a galaxy varies, but assuming there was an average of hundred billion stars per galaxy, that would mean there are about one trillion stars in the observable universe.

Also, within 13.7 billion light years, we can observe about fifty billion galaxies, each with roughly hundred billion stars.

HOW GREAT THOU ART

While enjoying his walk, Carl Gustaf Boberg—a pastor, editor, and member of the Swedish Parliament—would capture the words to *How Great Thou Art*, after the storm was over.

A thunderstorm had suddenly appeared out of nowhere, a gusty wind began to blow, and Boberg looked over the clear bay and heard a church bell in the distance. Immediately, the words began to form in his heart;

O Lord, my God, when I in awesome wonder,
Consider all the worlds Thy Hands have made.
I see the stars, I hear the rolling thunder,
Thy power throughout the universe displayed

Then sings my soul, my Savior God, to Thee
How great Thou art, how great Thou art
Then sings my soul, my Savior God, to Thee
How great Thou art, how great Thou art.

Later, this poem was published in 1891 in "Witness of the Truth"—the weekly newspaper that Boberg edited. It was later translated in German.

In 1927, it was published in a Russian version of the German text. Stuart K. Hine, the English missionary to Ukraine, translated three stanzas into English, and sang it at an evangelistic meeting with his wife during World War One.

Considering the wonder of His creation, these words capture this awe-inspiring God.

SEED POSSESS THE GATES

A gate provides access or entrance to a place, but also serves as a deterrent to would-be encroachers and invaders.

In ancient times, cities were protected with walls and gates. Important business transactions were also conducted at the city gates.

Allowing entrance through gates meant authorized access to the territory. In Genesis 19:1, Lot welcomed two angels to Sodom at the city gate.

This was the first mention of city gate in the Bible. When David was king over Israel, he gave instructions to his military at the city gate.

Therefore, to control the gates of your enemies was to triumph over them. In Matthew 16:18, Jesus says;

"And I say also unto thee, that thou art Peter, and upon this rock I will build my church; and *the gates of hell shall not prevail against it.*"

By taking an oath, God was reassuring Abraham that through Christ, his seed would triumph and subdue their enemies.

We have been given the power and authority, as the seed of Abraham, to trample over the works of the enemy. We have dominion over all the power of the enemy through Christ.

The Church of Jesus Christ cannot be defeated, because, through Abraham's *Ultimate Sacrifice*, God guaranteed victory for the Church!

THE BLESSING OF ALL NATIONS

God's promise to bless the nations of the earth through the seed of Abraham was not a cock-and-bull story. It is as true today as it was then. It was to be fulfilled through Christ, the seed of Abraham.

The Bible states,

"For as many of you as have been baptized into Christ have put on Christ. There is neither Jew nor Greek,

there is neither bond nor free, there is neither male nor female: for ye are all one in Christ Jesus. And if ye be Christ's, then are ye Abraham's seed, and heirs according to the promise."
- Galatians 3:27-29

BECAUSE THOU OBEYED MY VOICE

Indeed, obedience is unequivocally better than sacrifice. To think that Abraham's act of obedience to God would result in promises of perpetual possession of a land, innumerable family, the defeat and annihilation of their enemies, and the blessing of all nations on earth, was inconceivable.

Yet, God tells Abraham,

"Because you obeyed my voice."

Clearly, choices have consequences. The choice to obey God, and to offer his son as his *Ultimate Sacrifice*, had endless blessings and wide-reaching benefits.

Not only was Abraham blessed, his seed was blessed as well. God blesses us so we can be a blessing. Giving back to others, especially the least privileged, is worship. The scripture says,

"And the King shall answer and say unto them, Verily I say unto you, inasmuch as ye have done it unto

one of the least of these my brethren, ye have done it unto me." - Matthew 25:40

It is astonishing that true worship would produce such a monumental impact. But then God reciprocates when we offer true worship.

There is a mammoth blessing associated with honoring God with our u*ltimate sacrifice*; although we do not worship God because we seek a blessing.

To worship God the way Abraham did, to the extent where he was willing to sacrifice his son as a burnt offering, will always attract God's utmost attention.

SUMMARY

Make a decision today to emulate Abraham's example. Remember, to make the ultimate sacrifice, we must begin with obedience.

It is the basis on which our sacrifice is acceptable to God. Take the time to prepare for the encounter, and remain sensitive to the Holy Spirit, as God gives directions in true worship.

Set the stage before you engage, and be sure to build an altar so you don't falter before the Rock of Gibraltar.

With society being gradually decimated by an epidemic of moral decadence, the New Testament believer must be conscious of the quality of the worship of God.

The *Ultimate Sacrifice* requires that we relinquish our rights and privileges, and not usurp or infringe God's absolute authority.

When Abraham learned to do this, there were two things God did that guaranteed a personal and generational blessing. First, God swore by Himself and then took an oath to honor His promise.

Furthermore, God dispatched the pre-incarnate Christ to the place of sacred worship, who supernaturally provided the sacrificial lamb.

Chapter 12
FINALE

In the Old Testament, the children of Israel had seven most common Hebrew words they used to describe the worship of God. Without listing them in any particular order, they are:

- *"Barak* – to kneel or bow, to give reverence to God as an act of adoration.
- *Halal* – to praise, to make a show of or rave about, to glory in or boast upon, to be clamorously foolish about your adoration of God.
- *Tehillah* – to sing halal; a new song, a hymn of spontaneous praise glorifying God in song.
- *Shachah* – to depress or prostrate in homage or loyalty to God, bow down, fall down flat.
- *Todah* – an extension of the hand, avowal, adoration, a choir of worshipers, confession, sacrifice of praise, thanksgiving.
- *Yadah* – to use, hold out the hand (to worship with extended hands).

- *Zamar* – to touch the strings or parts of a musical instrument."[33]

NEW TESTAMENT WORSHIP

Used 54 to 60 times in the King James Version of the Bible, the Greek word for worship is *proskuneo,* which means; *"to kiss the hand towards one, in token of reverence,"* or *"to fall upon the knee or prostrate to pay homage as an expression of profound reverence."* [34]

In a post Neo-Pentecostal era, *worship and praise* is expressed in diverse genres of music. Although *worship* songs are usually slow-paced, that does not necessarily constitute worship.

Worship has to be God-ward or vertical. Meaning no matter the genre, the words should be addressed directly to God. It must tell of who He is and of His worth.

---

[33] www.kevincook.com/worship/hebrew-words-for-worship
Cook, Kevin. "Hebrew words for worship, music, scripture, and worship." Copyright © 2015

[34] www.biblestudytools.com/lexicons/greek/kjv/proskuneo.html
The KJV New Testament Greek Lexicon Copyright © 2017, Jupiter Images Corporation

"The English word "worship" comes from two Old English words '*weorth*', which means *worth* and *scipe* or *ship*, which means something like *shape or quality.* So *worth-ship* is the quality of having worth or of being worthy."[35]

Therefore whether the music is reggae, calypso, afro-beat or heavy metal and characterized by guitars, strobe-lights or fog machines that *accentuate* the "worship" experience or not, the fundamental truth is that worship must address God and His worth.

Realizing times have changed; we have to respond with an avant-garde approach that is abreast with modern times, as long as we don't lose this essence. We must resist the temptation of waging war on style and focus on substance.

I am persuaded the story of Abraham provides us the template for fulfilling this herculean but noble task. Times may have changed but the tenets remain the same. Practice may have been modified, but the principles remain.

Dearly beloved,

---

[35] www.gci.org/God/worship
Morrison, Michael. What is worship?
©2016 Grace Community International

I pray you have been impacted by this book.

If we can engage this all-mighty God through the power of worship, giving Him our *Ultimate Sacrifice*, we will access great doors in our lives and those of our family and descendants as well.

Many times, worship is limited to singing melodic songs, but Abraham teaches us that it precedes and is above music. When there is no music, the New Testament believer should be able to worship anyway.

Abraham worshiped without music, yet God was moved and swore to bless him.

The Apostle Paul wrote to the church at Rome of two inseparable realities…*sacrifice and worship.* He sates,

"Therefore, I urge you, brothers and sisters, in view of God's mercy, to offer your bodies as a living sacrifice, holy and pleasing to God—this is your true and proper worship." - Romans 12:1.

Worship and sacrifice both find their place on the same side of a coin.

Conclusively, to worship is to offer sacrifice, as to offer sacrifice is to worship.